Filmguide to

8½

INDIANA UNIVERSITY PRESS FILMGUIDE SERIES
Harry M. Geduld and Ronald Gottesman,
General Editors

Filmguide to

8½

TED PERRY

INDIANA UNIVERSITY PRESS
Bloomington   London

FOR MIRIAM

Published in Canada by Fitzhenry & Whiteside Limited, Don Mills, Ontario
Manufactured in the United States of America

Library of Congress Cataloging in Publication Data
Perry, Ted, 1931–
   Filmguide to 8½.
   (Indiana University Press filmguide series)
   Bibliography
   1. 8½. [Motion picture] I. Title. II. Series.
PN1997.E366P4   791.43'7   74-27180
ISBN 0-253-39321-3
ISBN 0-253-39322-1 pbk.

contents

credits

8½

A film by	Federico Fellini
Produced by	Angelo Rizzoli for Cineriz (Rome) and Francinex (Paris)
Presented in the United States by	Joseph E. Levine, Embassy Pictures
Story by	Federico Fellini and Ennio Flaiano
Screenplay	Federico Fellini, Ennio Flaiano, Tullio Pinelli, Brunello Rondi
Director of Photography	Gianni Di Venanzo
Cameraman	Pasquale De Santis
Scenery and Wardrobe	Piero Gherardi
Assistant Director and Casting	Guidarino Guidi
Editor	Leo Catozzo
Make-up	Otello Fava
Music	Nino Rota
Sound Effects	Mario Faraoni, Alberto Bartolomei
Production Supervisor	Clemente Fracassi
Artistic Collaboration	Brunello Rondi
Production Director	Nello Meniconi
Assistants to the Director	Giulio Paradisi, Francesco Aluigi, Mirella Gamacchio (script girl)
Assistant Editor	Adriana Olasio
Assistant Director of Production	Alessandro von Normann
Production Assistants	Angelo Jacono, Albino Morandin, Mario Basili

Scenery and Wardrobe
Assistants   Luciano Ricceri, Vito Anzalone,
                                Orietta Nasalli Rocca, Alba
                                Rivaioli, Clara Poggi, Renata
                                Magnanti, Eugenia Filippo

8½ premiered in Italy in February 1963. The French premiere was in May 1963. On June 25, 1963, the film opened in New York City at the Festival and Embassy theatres. The American version of *8½* is two hours and fifteen minutes long.

CAST

Guido Anselmi	Marcello Mastroianni
Luisa Anselmi	Anouk Aimée
Carla	Sandra Milo
Claudia	Claudia Cardinale
Rossella	Rossella Falk
The Actress	Madeleine Lebeau
The Fashionable, Unknown Woman	Caterina Boratto
Gloria Morin	Barbara Steele
Mario Mezzabotta	Mario Pisu
Pace, the Producer	Guido Alberti
Conocchia	Mario Conocchia
Fabrizio Carini (Daumier)	Jean Rougeul
La Saraghina	Edra Gale
Maurice, the Magician	Ian Dallas
Guido's father	Annibale Ninchi
Guido's mother	Giuditta Rissone
The Cardinal	Tito Masini
The Cardinal's secretary	Frazier Rippy
The Cardinal's retinue	Comte Alfredo de la Feld and Sebastiano de Leandro
Guido's grandmother	Georgia Simmons
The nurses	Maria Raimondi and Marisa Colomber

The old peasant relative	Palma Mangini
The little girl at the farmhouse	Roberta Valli
Guido at the farmhouse	Riccardo Guglielmi
Guido as a schoolboy	Marco Gemini
Jacqueline Bonbon	Yvonne Casadei
Luisa's sister	Elisabetta Catalano
A friend of Luisa and Rossella	Rossella Como
Enrico	Mark Herron
The two girls on the bed	Eva Gioia and Dina De Santis
Cesarino, the production supervisor	Cesarino Miceli Picardi
Bruno Agostini, the production director	Bruno Agostini
The Black dancer	Hazel Rogers
Edith, the Model	Hedy Vessel
The production accountant	John Stacy
Miss Olympia (as Carla in screen tests)	Olimpia Cavalli
La Saraghina (in some screen tests)	Maria Antonietta Beluzzi
The Spa Doctors	Roberto Nicolosi
	Luciana Sanseverino
The American journalist	Eugene Walter
His wife	Gilda Dahlberg
The producer's girl friend	Annie Gorassini
Maya	Mary Indovino
The airline hostess	Nadine Sanders
A friend of Luisa's; also an old journalist	Matilde Calnan
The Cardinal in the screen tests	Comtesse Elisabetta Cini
One of the clowns in the parade	Polidor (Ferdinand Guillaume)
The Agent	Neil Robinson
Claudia's agent	Mino Doro

*Claudia's press
  representative*   Mario Tarchetti
The school president   Maria Tedeschi

Also with: Giulio Paradisi, Valentina Lang, Annarosa Lattuada, Agnese Bonfanti, Flaminia Torlonia, Anna Carimini, Maria Wertmüller, Francesco Ragamonti, Prince Vadim Wolkonsky, Grazia Frasnelli, Gideon Bachmann, Deena Boyer, John Francis Lane. The entire technical staff participated in the final circus dance scene.

outline

In a film which intends to confound periods of time and levels of experience, an outline of the content may seem confusing. The individual scenes are detailed chronologically as they appear in the American version of *8½*.

1. TUNNEL. A traffic jam. Greatly disturbed and feeling claustrophobic, Guido Anselmi crawls out of his car and floats above the other vehicles to the end of the tunnel.

2. THE SKY. Guido floats above the beach and water. He is pulled down by a rope attached to his leg, and then falls toward the ocean.

3. BEDROOM AND BATHROOM OF A SPA OR THERMAL RESORT. Guido awakens, surrounded by doctors and a nurse. Carini, a writer, enters and discusses the film Guido proposes to make.

4. THE SPA GROUNDS, BY DAY. Guido and others are queued up for dosages of mineral water. A girl (Claudia) dressed in white appears, as if in a dream, and offers the mineral water to Guido. The writer Carini criticizes Guido's idea for the film. Guido's old friend, Mario Mezzabotta, appears accompanied by his young mistress, Gloria.

5. RAILWAY STATION, BY DAY. The train arrives, bringing Carla, Guido's mistress.

6. DINING ROOM OF A HOTEL NEAR THE STATION. Guido and Carla arrive. They sit at a table as Carla talks and eats.

7. BEDROOM IN THE SAME HOTEL. Carla and Guido play games and make love.

8. CEMETERY. Guido's mother and father evade, taunt, and criticize him. The producer of Guido's film appears briefly. After helping his father down into a hole in the ground, perhaps his grave, Guido kisses his mother. When the embrace is broken, the mother has been transformed into Luisa, Guido's wife.

9–10. THE HALL OF THE SPA HOTEL. Guido walks along playfully. He enters an elevator containing a Cardinal and his retinue.

11. SPA HOTEL LOBBY. Guido is besieged by people who query him about the film he is making. He tries to avoid being specific. A French actress is particularly concerned about what role she will play. Claudia's manager wants to see a script. Guido dismisses several prospective actors who do not appear old enough. Pace, the producer, arrives.

12. SPA GROUNDS, BY NIGHT. Transformed into a nightclub, the area is filled with people dancing and with tables where people sit, eat, drink, and talk. Guido is again bombarded by questions that he avoids answering. The tone of the scene changes as Maya and Maurice appear with a demonstration of extrasensory perception. As a finale, they read Guido's mind. Maya writes "Asa Nisi Masa" on the blackboard, a phrase from Guido's childhood.[1]

13. A FARMHOUSE. The boy Guido is visiting his grandmother. He and several other children are bathed in a large vat of wine lees, then put to bed. One of the other children tells Guido that if he will only pronounce the magic words, "Asa Nisi Masa," a portrait on the wall will reveal a treasure to them.

14. THE SPA HOTEL LOBBY. The French actress tries again to get information about her role. Mezzabotta is playing the piano for Gloria. Guido speaks on the phone to his wife, Luisa.

15. A ROOM IN THE SPA HOTEL, equipped as a film production office. The staff is at work. Guido enters and takes note of what they are doing.

16. A HALL IN THE SPA HOTEL. One of Guido's production assistants, Conocchia, complains about the way he is treated.

17. GUIDO'S BEDROOM IN THE SPA HOTEL. Guido tries to specify what role Claudia will play. She appears in the room, performing some of the roles his imagination suggests. There is a transition in time, and Guido is awakened by the phone. Carla is sick.

18. CARLA'S BEDROOM IN THE HOTEL TERMINAL. She is feverish. Guido tries to comfort her but soon turns his attention to thoughts of what he will say to the Cardinal at a meeting the next day.

19. THE SPA GROUNDS. The two subordinates of the Cardinal take Guido to meet the church official. Before Guido can ask any questions, the prelate asks about Guido's marriage and then discourses about the mournful singing of the birds. Guido turns his head and in the same area where he earlier saw Claudia descend to offer him mineral water, he now sees a large woman.

20. A SCHOOLYARD. The boy Guido is persuaded by some other boys to go with them to visit La Saraghina.²

21. A BEACH. La Saraghina dances a voluptuous rhumba for the boys. Some school officials arrive and drag Guido away.

22–26. SEVERAL ROOMS IN THE SCHOOL. Guido is condemned by the officials of the religious school and his mother. He is punished in front of his peers and told in the confessional that La Saraghina is the devil. He leaves the confessional and kneels before a statue of the Virgin.

27. THE BEACH. The boy Guido kneels and waves to La Saraghina.

28. THE SPA HOTEL DINING ROOM. Carini continues his criticism of the film director. In the background, the Cardinal tells a joke to his retinue.

29. UNDERGROUND STEAM BATHS. Hordes of people descend the stairs. A voice summons Guido to a meeting with the Cardinal. When Guido says that he is not happy, the Cardinal implies that happiness does not belong to this world.

30–31. A STREET NEAR THE SPA HOTEL AT NIGHT. Guido and others are walking. He meets Luisa, his wife, who has come to visit him at the spa. They dance together at an outdoor cafe.

32. THE SPACESHIP TOWER ON THE BEACH. As the producer, Pace, talks about the tower that Guido has had him build for the film, Guido bares his feelings to one of Luisa's friends, Rossella. He tells her that he is confused and uncertain.

33. GUIDO'S BEDROOM AT THE SPA HOTEL. Guido is already in bed when Luisa comes in. They have a violent argument.

34. AN OUTDOOR CAFE NEAR THE SPA HOTEL. Guido, Luisa, and Rossella are seated together, talking, when Carla arrives. Guido tries to deny to Luisa that he is having an affair with Carla. Luisa angrily denounces him. In what seems to be a moment of Guido's fantasy, Carla and Luisa dance together.

35. THE FARMHOUSE. The scene of Guido's childhood has now been transformed into a harem, where almost all of the women in Guido's life are present to bathe, comfort, and care for him. The women challenge Guido and he has to take a whip in hand to put them in order.

36. MOTION PICTURE THEATER. Guido, Carini, Luisa and her friends, Pace, and part of the production staff are present to screen some tests. When Carini continues to criticize, Guido imagines him to be hanged. As the tests are seen on the screen, Guido becomes even more troubled and confused. Pace presses him to decide about some of the roles. Luisa, troubled by what she sees as her double on the screen, leaves angrily. Claudia arrives and Guido leaves with her.

37–38. AN OLD PIAZZA. Guido and Claudia drive off together and stop in the middle of an old piazza, discussing the film, the part she might play, Guido, and the film's protagonist. Just as Guido admits to her his own misgivings and confusion, that there is no part for her and that indeed there is no film, a number of cars enter the piazza and members of the production staff announce that the producer has called a press conference for the next day.

39. THE PRESS CONFERENCE ON THE BEACH BESIDE THE SPACE-SHIP TOWER. Pace is trying to use the press conference to announce the beginning of the film. Unfriendly faces and voices bombard Guido with questions about the film. He climbs under the table and there is the sound of a gun shot.

40. THE SPACESHIP TOWER ON THE BEACH. The tower is being dismantled. Carini says that Guido has done the right thing to cancel the picture. Maurice appears and Guido senses a change in his own feelings. Almost all of the people with whom Guido has been associated now appear, dressed in white. Grabbing a megaphone, Guido gathers them together for a dance around a circus ring. The child Guido appears and pulls back a curtain drawn accross one portion of the tower. The other persons in Guido's life descend the tower staircase and join in the dance. Motion picture spot lights are trained on the ring. Luisa appears and reluctantly joins him in the dance around the ring. The characters dance off, leaving only three clowns and the boy Guido who, still playing his flute, is the last to depart from a tiny circle of light.

the director

Federico Fellini was born on January 20, 1920, in Rimini, a small town on the Adriatic coast of Italy. His father was a salesman, and the family included a sister and a brother. At an early age Fellini was sent to a religious boarding school whose strict discipline deeply disturbed him. Once he came upon a circus and stayed for several hours before being returned to the school. After high school Fellini made drawings for tourists on the beach at Rimini in a shop he called "Phoebus."

He then went on to Florence and Rome, where he held a variety of jobs, including a stint as a cartoonist. With the support of the actor Aldo Fabrizi, with whose company he toured briefly as a gagman or gag sketch writer, Fellini began writing for the radio and the cinema. He continued to work as writer, gagman, cartoonist, actor, and journalist through the war years. In 1943 he met and married Giulietta Masina, who later was to star in a number of his films. When the Allied Forces entered Italy, Fellini briefly ran a shop where an American soldier could be caricatured or photographed or have a record made of his voice.

During this period, Fellini met Roberto Rossellini, who was to be a profound influence upon his life. From 1944 to 1949, he worked as writer and assistant director with Rossellini and a number of other Italian directors, such as Zavattini, Lattuada, Germi, De Sica, and Blasetti.

In 1950, Fellini and Alberto Lattuada codirected *Variety Lights* and the career of the young man from Rimini was underway. The film follows the life of a small troupe of music hall performers down on its luck. In his first film directed alone, *The White Sheik* (1952), Fellini was already showing his interest in the discrepancy between kinds of reality. The story concerns a young woman in Rome on her honeymoon who slips away to search for the White Sheik, a character in a *fumetti*—an Italian comic strip composed of actual photographs. She finds the model and discovers that he is nothing like the fictional hero. (The story was by Michelangelo Antonioni, who had himself made a short film about the *fumetti, L'amorosa menzogna,* 1948.)

Fellini's next film, *I vitelloni* (The Loafers, 1953) drew extensively on his experiences as a young man in a small town, observing and mingling with young men who had little purpose in life. In the same year he made *The Matrimonial Agency,* an episode in the composite film, *Amore in città* (Love in the City).

With his next picture, Fellini attracted international attention. It was *La strada* and the cast included Anthony Quinn and Richard Basehart as well as his wife, Giulietta Masina, who gave an engaging performance. As in most of his films, Fellini was heavily involved in creating the original story and writing the screenplay.[3] *La strada* has much in common with other Fellini films—a travelling act, a circus, the need to love and be loved, the strength of weakness.[4] Quinn played a carnival strong man who all but buys a gentle retarded girl from her family to serve him in his travels. She is stimulated by her experiences and blooms under his attention, brutish and unloving as it is, until the end of the film, when it is the strong man who discovers what he has lost in leaving her alone in the mountains.

For American audiences, the chronology of Fellini's work is sometimes confusing, since his early films found their way across the Atlantic somewhat after their European release. *La strada* was finished in 1954 but not shown in the United States until 1956, when it won an Academy Award for best foreign language film of the year.

In 1955, Fellini completed *Il bidone* (The Swindle), starring Broderick Crawford and Richard Basehart, about several con men who often operate in disguise—as clergymen, for instance. Again, there is the discrepancy between appearance and reality, the sadness of lives without meaning.

The same themes are prominent in *The Nights of Cabiria,* finished in 1956 and the 1957 Academy Award winner for best foreign language film. Giulietta Masina, who had a number of roles in previous films, again was the central character, a prostitute who is swindled out of her savings by a man who pretends to love her. The ending is in many ways similar to that of *8½* and other Fellini films. Bereft of her savings and her supposed lover, Cabiria walks down a road when a group of young people come upon her, playing music, dancing, and singing. In a moment of pure grace, they help her to smile despite what has happened. There is a scaffold structure near Cabiria's shack like the rocket tower in 8½. *Nights of Cabiria* begins and ends with Cabiria being cheated by a supposed lover, the kind of circular structure that recurs in Fellini's films. The visual analogy is the dance, especially the dance around a ring that concludes 8½.[5]

Fellini's international reputation was firmly established by his next film, *La dolce vita,* which he finished in 1959 and which was given its United States premier in 1961. Focusing on the sweet, sad life of a group of upper middle class and aristocratic Romans, who waste their days and nights with activities which even to them seem empty, the film reminds the viewer of concerns Fellini showed in *I vitelloni. La dolce vita* also revealed Fellini's increasing willingness to disregard conventional narrative forms, for the film moves from episode to episode with little concern for cause and effect. Although it was not so obvious at the outset, this episodic form had always been characteristic of Fellini's work, discernible even as far back as *Roma, città aperta* (Rome, Open City) and *Paisan,* two of the Rossellini films that Fellini worked on. In the formal development of Fellini's films, the episodic structure becomes more and more apparent; it is the formal core of 8½, *Satyricon,* and to a lesser extent, *Amarcord.*

During the period before 8½, Fellini completed *The Temptations of Doctor Antonio,* a sketch for the film *Boccaccio '70,* which was released in the United States in 1962. The subject of the sketch is one that has always attracted Fellini—the pretense of morality. Dr. Antonio is affronted by an enormous billboard of Anita Ekberg and tries to have it destroyed. But the billboard comes to life—larger than life—and pursues him. Dr. Antonio succumbs, almost too willingly, to Anita's giant charms.

After completing 8½ in 1963, Fellini directed his wife in *Juliet of the Spirits* (1965), a film which in many ways was the female counterpart of 8½. The film explored a woman's response to many of the problems which Guido dealt with in 8½. There were important differences, however, among them Fellini's use of color to create the particular emotional world through which Juliet moves. But her problems have less to do with her vocation and more to do with an unfaithful husband and a past which she cannot clearly understand.

The ending of the picture is similar to *8½* and *The Nights of Cabiria* as Juliet arrives at an understanding and acceptance of herself through an act of grace.

Toby Dammit was a sketch completed by Fellini in 1967. The short film illuminated in a nightmare fashion some of the same concerns of *8½*. It is one of the few Fellini films based on a previously written story, in this case Edgar Allan Poe's "Never Bet the Devil Your Head." Terence Stamp plays an unstable English actor who flies to Italy to star in the first Christian western. He is given the sports car that is to be his fee and drives drunkenly through the night. In the end he is decapitated by an unnoticed low barrier cable as he tries to jump a washed-out bridge; a little girl in white, first seen bouncing her ball at the Rome airport, appears on the other side.

Fellini's Satyricon was completed in 1969. Based loosely upon Petronius Arbiter's story of ancient Rome, the film is a moving fresco of a world so distant and removed from contemporary civilization that every gesture, every sound, every sight seem unique, as if made for the first time before the viewer's eyes. The film has been called a "documentary of a dream;" it is a series of sketches loosely tied together by the journey of Encolpius. Fellini's early attraction for the more subjective aspects of human experience is given full rein in *Satyricon*. An act of the imagination, it is presented on the screen without benefit of an interlocutor.

His next two films, *The Clowns* and *Roma,* seem more relaxed. *The Clowns,* released in America in 1971, was originally made for Italian television. It depicts the lives of the great clowns, inside and outside the arena, treating Fellini's concern with the difference between appearance and reality. *Roma* explores Fellini's own feelings about the city of Rome, contrasting the city of today and the city he found when he first arrived during the Fascist period. With *The Clowns* and *Roma,* Fellini stepped back into a semi-documentary style, showing the filmmaking process as an integral part of each film.

This exposure of the filmmaking process may have seemed at the time to be something new in Fellini's work. It was not, however. In *Variety Lights* a great deal of attention was paid to the difference between the lives of the troupe and their performance on the stage. With its exploration of the difference between the actual White Sheik and the *fumetti* White Sheik, Fellini exposed a similar difference between illusion and reality. And even in *Nights of Cabiria,* especially in the scene where Cabiria is hypnotized in the music hall, the viewer is very much aware of the audience, Cabiria on stage, and the off-stage activities—the spotlight striking the lens, the cast and crew lounging in the wings. The presentation of the director and crew in *The Clowns* and *Roma* were extensions and elaborations of concerns already evidenced in earlier films, not the least of which is *8½* itself.

Amarcord, released in Italy during December 1973, was a return in many ways to the subject matter and style of earlier Fellini works, recalling as it does the world, time, and way of life Fellini himself experienced in a small town on the Adriatic coast. It is apt that *Amarcord* means (in the local dialect) "I remember," since so much of Fellini's work has been concerned with his own life, either in the form of willed recollection or insistent psychic pressures of dream and nightmare. From his experiences in Rimini, to his feeling for the city of Rome, through his various occupations, to the crises of middle age, his films and his life are closely interwoven.

Yet it is unfair to charge that his films are merely autobiographical statements: their popularity shows that they transcend his own experience. What has delighted the viewers of Fellini's films has often been the peculiar intensity with which he presents his view of the world. Viewers see their own world from a fresh vantage point or, at the very least, see a world which is the unique vision of an exquisitely sensitive person and are able to share it.

In this respect, *8½* is peculiarly important, for it seems to be the most directly presented autobiographical statement of all—the crisis of a film director who is confronted with the problems of middle age, confusion over the film he is making, a marriage that is breaking up. Also interesting about *8½* is its formal structure and the relationship of that structure to the director's earlier and later films.[6] It is a film that stands midway in Fellini's body of work, retaining some semblance of a story and yet reaching forward toward those films like *The Clowns* and *Roma* which make the filmmaking process part of their subjects.

the production

Fellini seems to have begun formulating his ideas about *8½* early in 1960, but the actual shooting did not begin until May 9, 1962; it was completed on October 14, 1962. Fellini had visited Chianciano, a thermal resort north of Rome, in autumn 1960 and decided to take it as the basis for the setting of *8½*. By late 1960, he had already begun to formulate the basic outline[7] of the film. Its working title was chosen because he had previously directed seven-and-a-half films, counting episodes of other films and the work codirected with Lattuada. The title is the equivalent of an opus number.

When shooting began, almost all the sets were constructed either at the Titanus-Appia Studios in Rome or in the section of the city where Mussolini's ill-fated Esposiozione Universale di Roma (EUR) was to have taken place. The lobby of the spa hotel, the underground steam baths, the church school, and several other scenes were done in one of the EUR buildings. The wall and platform where the patients come for mineral water and where the night club dancing and performances take place were constructed in the EUR woods. On the nearby Cecchignola military reservation's firing range, the cemetery, the street of the resort, and the outdoor cafe were all constructed. The narrow piazza where Claudia and Guido talk at the end of the film was filmed on location at Filacciano, a small sixteenth-century village north of Rome. The train station where Guido meets Carla was filmed on the Via Prenestina in Rome. The large Roman studios of Cinecittà were used for some process shooting, and the movie theater interior was shot in Tivoli at the Italia Theater. A school in Viterbo, fifty miles outside Rome, was used for the courtyard of young Guido's school, and the beaches between Ostia and Fiumicino were the sites of the tower and the scenes with La Saraghina. All the other shooting was done at the Titanus-Appia Studios, often referred to as Scalera.

Few problems were encountered in the actual shooting of *8½*, although as with his hero, Fellini waited until the last minute to make some decisions (such as casting Sandra Milo as Carla) and he seems to have been deliberately vague (or unsure) about the film's content, even during the shooting. Supposedly only Mastroianni among the cast was allowed to read the script. Many members of the cast were nonprofessionals whom Fellini chose for the film. Another ending was initially shot and then discarded. It involved a scene in the dining car of a train. All the people of Guido's past were there, sitting at the tables and dressed in white. He came to the same realizations about himself, accepted himself for what he was, and reached a tentative reconciliation with his wife. This and other cut scenes can be found in the French or Italian scripts noted in the bibliography.

analysis

8½ is the film of *8½* being made; *the 'film in the film' is, in this case, the film itself.*
—Christian Metz

In *8½* Fellini clearly shows himself to be what we have always at least half suspected him of being, a baroque fantasist whose private world has nothing more than a few accidents of time and place in common with any "real" world.
—John Russell Taylor

It seems to me that this must be my *mythos:* to try and throw off my back the upbringing I have had; that is, to try and uneducate myself in order to recapture a virginal availability and a new type of personal, individual education.
—Federico Fellini

Regardless of their form, Fellini's films have been intimately concerned with mental processes, with human subjectivity, the felt response of the individual *persona* to itself and the world. That is why writers discussing Fellini's world have so often resorted to words like dream, document of a dream, science fiction, nightmare, surreal, and fantasy. *8½,* with *Last Year at Marienbad,* was among the first commercial feature-length films to abandon the relations between the film experience and ordinary expectations of time, place, and sequence.[8]

One of the chief ways in *8½* that Fellini lifts viewers away from their usual concern with plot and meanings is to show the filmmaking process and to entwine it with the film being seen to the point that the two become inseparable. During many scenes of the film, the sound stage buzzer intrudes; there are bright set lights in Guido's bathroom; the rear of the set is exposed in the hotel lobby; lights, cameras, and technical crew are present in the final scene; in the piazza scene, Claudia comments on Guido's costume and makeup. Such things make it impossible to separate the film being planned, being shot, or being shown—"*8½* is the film of *8½* being made."[9] Thus are viewers led away from issues of subject matter and into direct experience with the form of the film, an experience in which the sensuous material celebrates the processes of the mind.

The crux of subjectivity in Fellini's films often concerns escaping the fate of the world. There are the strange structures in *Cabiria* and *8½*, the recurring disguises in the films, the frequent allusions to flying, the repeated acts of unexplained grace and unexplained miracles which seem to resolve the problems of living. There are recurring angels and other creatures that fly—even as Guido does in the opening of *8½*.

In its subjectivity, *8½* goes beyond the use of such obvious dream images to use basic dream modes of narrative. It leaps from event to event according to internal principle and not external narrative convention, and it confounds the world of the dreamer with the dream he is dreaming. In its interaction of memory and fantasy and present tense, *8½* seems to be a rendering of a mind trying to see, know, and reflect upon itself, to utter (or "other") itself into some palpable form.

The film continually displays Fellini's affection for the extraordinary visual statement, preferably in motion. *8½* relies heavily on movement in all its variant forms—camera, people, cutting, music, eye attention. In some scenes the camera moves incessantly, to pick up a minute detail, to enjoy a face that has never been seen before but which absolutely expresses a certain personality, to reveal a new perspective, to displace foreground with background. There is no way to describe Fellini's visual sense verbally: the similarity is perhaps to music. It is almost as if the lack of flow of notes in a piece of serial music were somehow translated into a visual flow evoking as powerful an emotional response. Surprising notes and disquieting chords find equivalents in the unusual and resonating details that Fellini juxtaposes to create his unique, exciting *mise-en-scène*. He undoubtedly has one of the most extensive visual palettes in the cinema.

The sense of movement in *8½* is also created by the rapid displacement of one space by another, not only through camera movement but also by the continual changing of scenery and locale. Few spaces are used more than once, and then in different contexts and lighting. The shifting locales are used to stress different feelings, and many transitions involve changes in mode of experience. Viewers may be confused as to where they are at the beginning of a scene; the point, of course, is not to pose a puzzle to unravel but to confound the levels of experience and to involve the viewer in the process.

Throughout the film, viewers are made to feel the situation as Guido experiences it. At times the camera movement traps Guido in the frame and, no matter where he goes, he is transfixed in its attention while other people are allowed freely to enter and exit frame, to be revealed and then disappear. At other times the camera may lose Guido, assuming its own personality and moving gratuitously. In the press conference, for instance, it often moves freely through the chaotic scene. More typically, the camera will assume Guido's point of view so that people can stare into it, harass it, accost it. This identification of Guido and the camera point of view, the self-referential ("mirror construction") nature of the film's form, and the camera movement that continually suggests something fearful off-screen, are the dominant strategies of the film.

Satyricon is the pinnacle of Fellini's progression into something more and more like documents of dreams and even science fiction. After it, the celebration of individual subjectivity takes more complex and subtle forms. The exposure of the camera, Fellini, and the business of filmmaking in *The Clowns* and *Roma* are variations of the same purpose.

Although *8½* is a transitional film in Fellini's work, revealing its process of taking form as content more readily than the others, it is unique and merits study for its own qualities. The man pinned in its view is in the midst of a middle-age crisis in which his creativity is paralyzed. In the course of trying to work out of his entrapment, he undergoes a primary process in which he regresses deeper and deeper into a desire for the liberation, spontaneity, comfort, and freedom from decisions that childhood and certain mother figures represent. The process takes the form of dreams, fantasies, and memories. He dreams to redeem himself. His relations to women are crucial to the evolution of the narrative—to simplify perhaps too neatly, Luisa (the wife) and the mother are distant and critical; Carla, La Saraghina, the nurse, and the early Claudia are there unequivocally to love, envelop, and care for him.

The film ends in a celebration which is not necessarily a solution to the problems it has posed. Guido's final conversation with Luisa is tentative, but whatever the words, the tone of the last scene is one of involvement and action. As always, Fellini indicates his preference for

action over intellectualization. The strengths of *8½* are the fecundity
of invention, the extraordinary visual sense, and its creator's unique
imagination.

Nino Rota's musical score calls for special comment. Since in Italy
almost all sound, including voice, is added after shooting, the director
will often play a piece of music during shooting, perhaps on a phono-
graph, to give the cast and crew some feeling for the rhythm of the
scene (a common practice in the silent film era). Thus in the production notes of Camilla Cederna included in the Italian script, and in the
book on *8½* by Boyer, there are frequent references to specific pieces
of music: "The Sorcerer's Apprentice," "Fiesta," "Two Guitars,"
"Circus March," "Saber Dance," and many others which may or may
not appear intact on the final soundtrack. However, in the case of
Nino Rota's score, a number of the pieces which appear on the final
soundtrack do resemble, in some passage or other, other pieces of
music. To avoid confusion by trying to identify each piece of music in
the soundtrack, even what it might vaguely resemble, I have referred
to the selections which appear on the record identified as the soundtrack of the film (RCA International FSO-6). Where the soundtrack
obviously depends upon another piece of music, the record indicates
the composer's name and, where applicable, the original title. For con-
venience in identifying the music during the analysis of the film, I will
list the pieces as they are given on the record. It should be obvious to
everyone who knows the film and the record, however, that there are
discrepancies. In some cases the problem may be that the tune on the
record was obscured during the mixing of the soundtracks. Also, parts
of one piece on the record will appear in another selection on the same
record. The *8½* theme, for instance, has three different versions. Some
music, such as "Blue Moon," is also missing from the record. Moreover, the order of the music on the record does not match the order in
the film. Parts of one piece, such as the one called "Carlotta's Galop"
on the record, often appear as individual refrains elsewhere in the film.
Nevertheless, a listing of the themes and tunes as given on the record
will be useful as a reference for the analysis of the film, and this listing
is given in a discography at the end of this volume.

1. TUNNEL (INTERIOR).[10] The first and second scenes are an articulation of space and light. Guido, dressed in black clothing, is trapped

in a traffic jam in an enclosed, suffocating atmosphere of a dark tunnel. Its shadowy edges are filled with unfriendly people staring at him as if he were in a fishbowl. There is a faint glimmer of light at the end. Gradually he gets out into an open space, filled with bright light, clouds, air, and a sense of freedom and light. This movement, from suffocation in the dark to floating in the light is central to the film. The articulation of space and light may be seen as an articulation of fate: man caught, glued to the earth, versus man freed from the weight of the earth, flying among the clouds.

The viewer does not see the man's face until the third scene. The camera continually returns to the back of his head, observing from his point of view the tunnel world in which he is trapped. One camera movement, for instance, follows the man's glance as he looks screen left to two people frozen in their cars, then comes back to him to follow his arm screen right as he moves to wipe the window. There is a cut to the space farther right where a face frowns at the camera, which then pans back screen left to the man trapped in the car.

This to-and-fro panning movement is paradigmatic not only because it visually traps the man at the center of an environment which oppresses and suffocates him, but also because in panning beyond the borders of his body, it has revealed the off-screen space to be filled with hostile people, frightening shadows, unexpected and alien visages. The restless movement of the camera suggests a struggle for freedom. Since we see the world through his eyes both physically and psychologically, the identification of audience and protagonist is made from the outset.

I dwell upon this one camera movement because it is the first instance of the dollying and trucking that I have mentioned—in which Guido is trapped by a camera that moves with him constantly, caging him by its frame no matter where he moves, while unfriendly people freely enter and exit from off-screen space, making demands on him, accosting him. This camera technique is particularly evident in the outdoor scene at the spa, in the lobby of the spa hotel, in the steam baths of the spa when it is announced that the Cardinal will see Guido, and at the press conference. In all these instances, Guido is revealed as trapped and surrounded; and this feeling is in some cases accentuated by the camera's assuming his point of view almost entirely as people stare toward him (the camera).

In this first scene the feeling of the man being encircled and stared at is increased by the constant movement of the camera. In the first two minutes of the film there are at least twelve camera movements. Only a few shots are static. The feeling of enclosure is created not only by the traffic jam (as in *Roma*) but also by a moving camera which continually reveals an off-screen space filled with unexpected images. The sense of being bottled up is emphasized by the steam that fills the man's car, the bodies that are encased in the second story of a bus, and the sounds created by the man as he claws on the car window and tries to beat his way out of the machine. Some of the sounds are similar to those heard later in the underground steam baths.[11]

Gradually, however, with great effort, the man extricates himself from the car, reaches a plateau above the level of the other cars and begins to float forward, the camera panning up his body and then trucking screen right with him. There is a feeling of floating, of release, of moving up and emerging from the enclosed space of threatening shadows. Guido enters the sunlight, free of the weight of gravity.

2. SKY (EXTERIOR). Seen from below by the camera which is trucking screen right with him, Guido begins to emerge from the tunnel. He shields his eyes from the bright sun; the noise of steam which earlier seemed to threaten suffocation now segues to a strong sound of wind. The scene begins with a dissolve from the man floating out of the tunnel to his floating up into the air. Another dissolve accentuates the clouds and the sky. Still another dissolve momentarily reveals an enormous steel scaffolding, the same one that the viewer will see several times later in the film as the tower constructed for Guido's film. The sequence of shots and dissolves inextricably links the floating, free man, the clouds, the scaffolding, and the sky. The shot of the scaffolding is itself a floating shot; the camera seems to be hand-held, gradually moving through the sky like a floating body.

This euphoric feeling of release is only momentary, however, as the camera reveals that the floating figure is actually tied by the foot with a rope. A man holding the rope on the beach below is joined by another man (later in the film he will appear as Claudia's manager) who rides up on a horse. A medallion on his forehead implies some mystical powers and thus, when he pronounces, "Down, definitely down," the floating figure quickly plunges toward the water. As the descent begins, the camera reverses angle to a shot looking down upon the falling figure. The dream of flying, floating free of fate, of responsibility, of human context, is only passing. It is the familiar fantasy of the single self in a condition of idyllic drift. As the figure falls toward the water, the sound of a man gasping is heard on the soundtrack. The next scene will reveal the source of the sound, a man awakening ostensibly from a nightmare. This overlapping of sound is an early clue to the kind of overlapping of levels of experience that will be found throughout the film.

3. BEDROOM AND BATHROOM OF A SPA OR THERMAL RESORT (INTERIOR). The movement from the murkiness of the tunnel to the brightness of the sky is now reversed again as the next scene takes place in the dark interior of a bedroom. The first shot, over which the gasping sound continues, is taken from behind the head of a bed as a hand and arm dart into the frame foreground. The camera position is similar to that seen earlier in the back seat of the car. Behind the head of the man in bed, the camera pans first right and then left to doctors who are circling over the man, asking him about his health and his next film. Again, in the dark *art nouveau* bedroom, the man (whose face the viewer has yet to see) is trapped—this time by doctors and a nurse who probe him with questions, touch him, tap him, prescribe for him, contain him. This feeling of oppressive encirclement, of being pinned down, is emphasized as another man enters the room, circles to one side and sits down in a chair against a wall. He is the director's collaborator, Carini, a writer hired by the producer to help with the script. The sense of their relationship is captured in the imagery before the writer speaks in his cold and sarcastic tone. The writer is first seen through an *art nouveau* version of "classical" carvings on a glass room divider. Passing behind these images, he circles the room half way, sits, hunches over, demoniacally expels smoke from his nose, avoids Guido's eyes, and evades questions about the script. The writer remains in medium long shot, across the room, while Guido's shrouded head (the doctor has thrown the director's robe up over his head to examine his back) is seen in nearer close-up. The distance between the two men is firmly established, and one more character has been introduced as estranged from Guido, accusing him.

The dialogue of the scene tells us that Guido Anselmi is middle-aged, that he is trying to begin work on another film, that he has come to the spa for his health, at least in part, and perhaps to shoot some of the new film. One shot in this scene, subtly links all this together. It begins with a profile of Guido's leg as the doctor examines it; the camera then dollies in, following the doctor's hand, to his medical bag which rests on top of photographs strewn all over the bed. The doctor picks up one of the photographic stills being used to select actors and actresses for the film and comments upon it. A visual link is thus established by this continuous shot which ties together the director, his work, and his health (his psychological and pyschic state). It is a straightforward camera movement, although one which might take several hours to set up, but one which suggests several relationships.

After the doctors have completed their examination and the writer has pronounced the results of his examination of the script, the camera shifts to a wider, reverse angle shot of the full room and Guido arises from the bed to walk toward the camera, sluggishly pulling on his robe. He walks down a shaft of light pouring through a window at the rear. The writer sits in the shadows on one side of the shaft of light. With the doctors circling in the background shadows, pronouncing their prescriptions for medicine and rest, Guido is again presented in the middle of dark shadows, a man surrounded. He is caught halfway through the journey of his life, sick, lost in something very much like a dark cave.

The camera cuts from this wide shot of the room to a low angle of an oval mirror, then moves in to a close-up of the mirror as Guido enters suddenly from off-screen. As his face becomes visible, there is a burst of music. It is Wagner's *Ride of the Valkyries,* used again during the revolt in Guido's harem and so identified on the record as "Rivolta nell'Harem." The music continues under this scene and is carried over into the next, where it is revealed that the music is actually being played by the orchestra outdoors at the spa. But since the viewer does not know this during the present scene, the music conspires to make the scene disquieting, subverting its illusionistic quality. The camera movement into the mirror, the introduction of a strong musical stinger, the turning on of the light, all occur mockingly at the moment when the viewer and Guido, in the context of the film, see his face, fully and in close-up. The strong emphasis upon the revelation of the man's face, finally, and the man looking at that face, with its tired, baggy eyes, the expression of utter disdain and contempt, places before the viewer the central concern of the film: Guido's confrontation with himself, in particular with the image of himself, an image created from the expectations and judgments of others.

The bathroom scene does much more than just introduce this theme. Even in such a simple matter as the attention to the black and white contrasts, as in the tiles of the bathroom, the scene introduces a motif which will recur throughout the film, for example, Guido's dark suit and Claudia's white dress.[12] The startling thing about the bathroom scene, however, is the way in which it introduces elements not quite right if the viewer were witnessing only one level of experience. For instance, when the lights come on in the bathroom, they are too bright and the sound is out of proportion, much like the buzz made when motion picture arc lights are first switched on. When the telephone begins to ring, it is unrealistically loud, and the sound is like that heard as a signal for quiet on certain movie studio sound stages. The viewer will hear that sound several times in the film. Here, it is merely irritating and out of place. But together with the annoying buzz of the arc lights and their brightness, the effect is disturbing, speaking of the scene as an event in the film and also about the process of filmmaking itself.

The disquieting effect is further compounded by Guido's reaction to the phone. It is obviously irritating to him, another intrusion from the outside world which he is trying to avoid, and he responds in a strange way, by lowering his body progressively in response to each ring. In the context of a film which has just stressed the difference between man trapped by gravity and man floating free in the sky, the gesture calls attention again, in a more humorous way, to a man being drawn downward and inward. Guido's impulse is to retreat to a foetal condition.

The lights are too bright, the sounds too loud, not only because of Guido's physical condition, but obviously because of his psychic condition. It was possible before to assume, given a few clues, that the tunnel and sky scenes were a nightmare (one level of experience) and that the bedroom scene was the true, present tense "reality." But now the bathroom episode has destroyed that comfortable division between levels of experience and suggests that the divisions are not as neat as the viewer might expect. This suggestion will be picked up again and again during the course of *8½*.

4. SPA GROUNDS, BY DAY (EXTERIOR). As the scene changes to the outdoor woods, where people are gathered to sun themselves and to queue up for their ration of mineral water, the Wagnerian music takes on more intensity, eventually changing to Rota's mixture of Rossini and Tchaikovsky, "Concertino alle terme." The viewer now discovers that the music is being played by a small orchestra on the grounds.

As Guido awaits his turn in one of the lines, he sees a young woman (Claudia) dressed in white, her hands folded across her chest, moving down out of the woods to where she can offer Guido a glass of water. She seems to float as she moves and the camera follows her, first in a medium long shot and then much closer. As noted earlier, that floating has special meaning for Guido. There are several cues, of course, that the event is something Guido imagines—the sudden interruption of the music while Claudia is present, the difference in the background behind Guido, and even the way in which Guido pulls his glasses down on his nose to look at her.

Parenthetically, a critic is tempted to discuss at length the use of glasses, sunglasses, and water throughout *8½*. Sometimes, for instance, taking off or putting on or moving glasses on the nose seems to be an obvious cue to some change in the character's insight. Certainly there is a very strong thread throughout the film which often deals with Guido's propensity for lying: when Guido touches his nose, one thinks of Pinocchio and his revealing nose. By the same token, a great deal of emphasis is given to various aspects of water: Claudia and Guido drive near running waters, Guido pours water on his head in the bathroom, he has come to "healing waters," La Saraghina's place and the tower are beside the sea. But as in so much of Fellini's work, the use of glasses or the meaning of water or white dresses or whatever is not consistent. Fellini jokes with us and with himself. Sometimes, in a very specific context, the critic can point to some particular meaning being evoked, but it is dangerous to make generalizations. What can be said is that the film is deeply concerned with truth and falsehood, with the relationship of water[13] and healing (salvation).

Claudia's appearance is a case in point. The meaning of the scene is the overall effect created by the simplicity of her dress, her smile, the floating quality created by her movement and the camera movement, and Guido's reaction. He sees, or remembers, or imagines, someone who offers him water. He takes great pleasure in her, in the way she moves, in the way she looks, in what she offers him. It is a moment of day-dreamt ecstasy, visualized in the form of a woman, something abstract and perhaps idealized, something he needs and wants, or so he seems to think at that moment.

Just the reverse is true of Carini, the writer whose criticism is resumed shortly after Guido has been awakened from his vision of

Claudia. Guido is again being prodded about his proposed film and its philosophic premise. For Guido that way of working seems impossible, however much his present paralysis may lead him to be influenced by Carini. He would like to listen to Carini, or so he tells himself, but actually he prefers spontaneous, intuitive action.

The appearance of Mario Mezzabotta, an old friend of Guido's, comes at that propitious moment when Guido is unsuccessfully trying to answer Carini. Indeed, there are a number of moments in the film when Guido, for one reason or another, fails to answer some direct questions put to him—about his script, about a person's role, about the film rushes. There is a pattern of Guido avoiding direct encounters or of fate luckily intervening to help him avoid them. That is his plight, of course; he is unwilling or unable, as Rossella will say later, to choose—which persons to cast, how to use the tower, when to start the film, what the film is, whether or not he has lost his inspiration.

Mezzabotta, on the other hand, has made a very decisive choice. He has left his wife of thirty-one years and is at the spa with a young girl, Gloria. She seems part wood nymph and part sorceress. As she approaches the camera, beginning to speak about the bee and the flower, a section from "Dance of the Mirlitons" accentuates the appearance of her face from under her hat. When Gloria sits down and presents her shapely legs for viewing, that is the moment she ironically selects to reveal the title of her university thesis: "The Plight of Modern Man As Reflected in the Contemporary Theater." Everything about her is just a little too obvious. But Mario and Gloria reflect Guido's problems. Mario has made a decision, and his decision involves dealing with his middle-age crisis in and through a younger woman. Guido, too, finds that his crisis involves women—his mistress, his wife, his remembered mother, La Saraghina, Claudia, several actresses. If he is to be a whole man, he must be so sexually as well as psychically.

During all this, the camera has not been still. First, until Carini and Guido sit down, the camera is relentlessly moving—long trucking shots, dolly movements, up and down boom movements. The camera speeds across the grounds, catching the faces of the people, their movements. Certain camera movements play with foreground and background by pulling a foreground action into the frame, sometimes even from the off-screen space below, and then pushing the foreground activity out of the frame to reveal and emphasize action in the background. The effect is to call attention emphatically to the off-screen world.

The camera movement is closely choreographed with the movement of people. As a man turns and moves in a certain direction, the camera follows him as if his movement determined the movement of the camera. Indeed, most of the camera movement here is so motivated. (In some other scenes the camera moves of its own accord, not following any movement on the screen.)

Rare and therefore the more disquieting are those camera movements which are gratuitous,[14] especially when such movement suddenly pulls into the frame from off-screen an unexpected sight, such as the conductor of the orchestra. As in the scene in the tunnel, this unexpected thrust into the frame throws the viewer off-guard and reminds him again that even in such a simple scene, the frame line is not sacred and the off-screen space is always to be reckoned with. Like the ringing of the telephone in Guido's bathroom, the outside world beyond the frame can and does intrude itself at any time.

This continual camera movement provokes other resonances, too. First, the choreography of people and camera movement, coupled with the music, accentuates the inexorable movement of time itself. There is a feeling that nothing can stop the rapid acceleration of time passing. The lively camera is ironically juxtaposed with the images of so many aging people, moving slowly and decrepitly around the grounds, marching one slow foot at a time to obtain their doses of mineral water. The presence of these aging people suggests that one of the themes of the film is aging; Guido would at times like to return to some of the things and states he enjoyed as a child. "You would like to live another hundred years" is the thought of the aging lady as revealed by Maya. "They're not old enough," Guido says, referring to the men his assistant has brought to play the part of the father. "You're not the man you used to be," Conocchia says to Guido.

The most dramatic aspect of the use of the camera in this particular scene is that the shots seem to be taken from Guido's point of view. People look directly into the camera (even more than they did in the tunnel): they giggle at it and turn away; one person even waves at the camera.

The camera-as-Guido occurs not only in the long opening shot of the scene, where the camera trucks by several people who look at Guido (directly into the camera) but also in numerous other places in the scene. In the conversation where Mario introduces Gloria and the group moves as they talk, the moving camera is closely identified with Guido's direct point of view. The long exchange between Carini and Guido, in which Carini walks beside the moving camera (Guido) and talks toward it, is another example. Having identified the camera point of view and Guido, the viewer is surprised to see, as the camera stops and pans screen right, that Guido is seated down in the frame. Through use of the subjective camera, with people staring and making demands directly into it, the pressure mounts upon the director and all those who have identified with him.

The setting and the people can hardly be characterized as anything other than comic. It is not burlesque, but comedy which celebrates life—in all its curious, disproportionate, humorous, unusual details.[15] What could be more pathetically comic than a man in a state of spiritual crisis taking himself among aging, sick, dying people, queuing up like them to receive "healing waters?" The frequent discrepancy in dress and music helps to accentuate both the comic and the pathetic aspects of Guido's crisis. He finds himself surrounded not only by older people but also by music and costumes that belong to an earlier era. These discrepancies are particularly apparent in the nightclub sequence and when the people are standing in line for their dosage of water.

5. RAILWAY STATION, BY DAY (INTERIOR). At the end of the previous scene, Guido was heard reading some of Carini's criticisms of his script. Now, in the railroad station he continues to read those remarks and then throws them to the ground in a disgusted rejection of the sterility and destructive intellectual analysis that Carini is trying to impose upon him. There is the sound of an approaching train. The camera trucks screen right to follow Guido as he moves toward the tracks which eventually line up directly in front of the camera. The train station itself, a bright, white tunnel (the opposite of the opening scene), is a pleasant creature of the imagination, bordering on make-believe. In the foreground, black wrought iron grill work supports flowers placed right and left of the track. This particular arrangement reminds one of a church, the aisle being replaced by a train track, the train bringing the bride, Carla. On the walls are posters about drinking, showing aged people.

Guido's willingness to walk off and forget his mistress, Carla, when he thinks she has not come, reveals how little this relationship really means to him. There is a boyish naivete in his willingness to bring Carla to the spa, then later to invite his wife. When he discovers that Carla really has arrived, he is terribly anxious about being seen with her. This fear is magnified in one shot where he circles back and forth behind her, as the camera pans to and fro, almost wishing that he could hide her with his body. His embarrassment is further revealed by his reaction to her excessive luggage and his timid explanation of why he has put her up in a small hotel other than his own.

Carla herself is impervious to his anxiety. She is there to serve as the uncritical mistress, a reflection of the attitudes displayed by such earth mother figures as La Saraghina and the nurses at the farmhouse.

6. DINING ROOM OF THE HOTEL TERMINAL BY DAY (INTERIOR). Guido has taken Carla to a small hotel near the railroad station. It has a "family" atmosphere and obviously cheap, since the train station whistles are so easily heard that it must be very near to the station.

Apart from her sensuality and her child-like enthusiasm, Carla seems to have little to offer to Guido. He reads his paper, hums a tune, and plays cards, while she rambles on about her husband, wanting Guido to get him a job. Guileless, she talks of her clothes, recalls a dream in which her husband kills Guido and herself with a broom. All these remarks, and others, are playful nonsense. The cutting of the shots is motivated almost entirely by what Carla says and does. Guido sits and waits, while she prattles and devours her chicken legs. The separation between them is indicated not only by their actions and dialogue at the table but also by the alternation of shots, first of one person and then of the other. The two of them are hardly ever seen within the same frame, nor is either seen from the other's viewpoint.

Very softly (so softly it is difficult to hear in 16mm prints), the viewer hears a tune being hummed in the background of the scene, perhaps by one of the people working at the hotel. It is the "Ricorda d'infanzia," which will be heard often again, particularly in the farmhouse of Guido's youth, in part of the harem scene, in part of a scene with La Saraghina, and when the men are tearing down the tower. The pattern is not absolutely clear but as the title suggests, the tune is to be identified with childhood memories and their accompanying feelings. Like the lullaby that it resembles, the tune is repeated several times when Guido fantasizes or remembers himself being cared for, lovingly smothered by an uncritical, accepting environment. Here the tune is readily associated with Carla, a creature who also recalls some of these same aspects of Guido's childhood.

7. BEDROOM IN THE SAME HOTEL, BY DAY (INTERIOR). Now Carla becomes for Guido what was suggested by her dress, her manner, her body, her eating of the chicken, her laughter, the humming of "Ricorda d'infanzia." Alone, in the darkened room, undressed, wrapped only in a sheet and wearing a black veil over her head, she plays his games with him, involves herself in totally uninhibited moments of near-magic and communion which seem in form and structure like La Saraghina's dance upon the beach, the children's bathing in the wine lees, the harem, the children's word games and magic.

For the moment it is Carla who allows Guido to do what he most wants to do, to escape his own fate here in the darkness of the room by pretending to be someone else. For the first time in the film, in the imaginary world the two people have created, Guido shows an ability to choose and act which has hardly been revealed before in the film. But there is a curious mixture of the active and the passive. By the end of the scene, Guido allows himself to be enveloped and smothered by Carla. The white sheet which Carla opens around her body resembles wings upon which she and Guido will fly, floating free above any reproachment or restraint, cut off from those prying, accosting faces. Their world of secrets and games is dark in its own right, and, unlike the period in the tunnel, the darkness is friendly, a way of escaping, closing themselves off from the world. If the earlier flight fantasized a soaring freedom for the spirit, Guido now play-acts an escape for the body.

The overall tone of the scene is playful, not sensual, erotic, or lustful. When the camera first follows Carla from window to mirror to another mirror, the viewer thinks the last mirror image to be a view of Guido on the bed. Fellini jokes with the viewer.[16] For a brief instant, Carla breaks the playful tone by asking, most seriously, what Guido would do if she really were a whore. Carla seems to have an unexpected level of seriousness and for a moment it stuns Guido. But when Carla comes back into the room, it is to laugh, to giggle, to take Guido's directions and fall upon him, smothering him with the sheets which resemble wings and the sheets in the farmhouse. She envelops him.

There is a dissolve to a later time in the same room. Guido is asleep in the foreground of the bed while in the background Carla eats peaches and reads something like a comic book. As the camera cuts to a very high angle shot of the same room, the viewer sees a woman moving sideways and waving a handkerchief. The shot suggests that the following sequence is what Guido might be dreaming as he lies in the bed. The two sequences overlap by having the woman present in Carla's bedroom. The visual overlap is similar to the sound overlaps which have already occurred, as when the viewer heard the gasp of Guido in bed while the figure was falling from the sky. For the most part, however, viewers are more accustomed, or less sensitive, to a sound overlap and the confusion of levels of experience which it implies. Now, in Carla's bedroom, they are asked to look at the beginning of the dream while also seeing the dreamer who is dreaming the dream. What clues at this point indicate that this is the beginning of a dream? The only formal change is the abrupt and extreme high angle shot. Carla seems not to notice the woman waving the handkerchief. And what clues are there to indicate which is the dream, the people in the bed or the woman waving a handkerchief? It is extremely important to see how the film has upset the causal order of experience, in a manner not that different from the earlier bathroom sequence, for instance. And it is also important to note that this particular scene in Carla's bedroom can be understood only in retrospect. That is, only upon seeing the next scene will the viewer have a clearer understanding of this scene. In *8½,* as with most worthwhile films, the experience of some present scene will reshape, in retrospect, the experience and understanding of some previous scene. Films collect meaning backwards as well as forwards.

8. CEMETERY, BY DAY (EXTERIOR). I write the title "cemetery" with some uncertainty. There is scant evidence that the viewer is looking at a cemetery. If it is indeed a cemetery, it is very much unlike more familiar ones. Guido would certainly avoid an actual cemetery. Yet there is a tomb and a hole into which the father eases himself. The overall tone of strangeness is supported by the music, "Cimitero," an uncomfortable dirge which will be echoed when Guido is in the steam bath, about to go to the Cardinal, and again in the harem scene when Jacqueline Bonbon goes upstairs; that is, "Cimitero" will later be heard in "Discesa al fanghi" and after "La Ballerina pensionata."

It is unnecessary to pursue each detail of the cemetery scene and its strange, empty, outdoor space. What is important, I think, is the overall feeling of Guido being estranged from his mother and father. Guido is actually absent from a number of shots, especially in the first part of the scene. The same technique is used elsewhere, usually to suggest estrangement and separation, as later in the film during the steam bath meeting with the Cardinal. Also, here in the cemetery scene, there is the evasiveness of the people. The mother walks away, the father runs behind a wall, the characters generally refuse to speak with Guido. They speak to him and at him but not with him. The estrangement and reproachment are emphasized by the subjective camera (a technique noted several times before), by the father's complaints about his tomb, by the producer's refusal to comment on how Guido is doing.

The mother doesn't answer Guido's questions, the father doesn't answer Guido's questions, the producer doesn't answer the father's questions, Guido doesn't answer the questions of Luisa, his wife. Luisa is quite alone in the last shot, a wide, high angle view of the entire lonely area. Guido is absent, as absent as he has been throughout much of the scene. The only time he is seen fully is when he is dressed in his schoolboy uniform. The parents separate themselves from one another and from their child. In being forced to play out the role dictated to him by his parents, the real Guido is as absent as when he is not present in the frame, elsewhere in the sequence. Throughout *8½* Guido confronts, and painfully has to deal with, alter egos which other people create in his place.

There is a similarity between this tomb, the interior of the car in the tunnel, the case in which the young Guido will later view the mummified saint, and the glass box in which the Fakir will be enclosed, seen briefly on the spa street. Moreover, special note should be taken of the identification of the mother and Luisa, evidenced by the exchange during the kissing. The producer is associated with Guido's father in the scene. Both of these associations are hints at a regressive or primary process at work in parts of the film, but even more properly they help the viewer to understand Guido's relationship with Luisa and the producer.

The overall impression of the scene is one of absence, of lack of communication, of reproachment, of estrangement, and of confusion on Guido's part. The camera helps to support this feeling by oblique angles and especially by gratuitous movement and cutting. Numerous cuts and camera movements have little or no conventional or ostensible motivation in the action. A particularly extreme example occurs when the camera, unmotivated, trucks screen left across the strange landscape and winds up on the tomb.

9. HALL OF THE SPA HOTEL (INTERIOR). As Guido walks down the hall, he seems positive, assertive, and his attitude is reinforced by the backward movement of the camera and Guido's actions. He whistles a sprightly tune (similar to parts of the Rossini section of "Concertino alle terme") and does a comic, clown-like dance step. On the one hand, Guido is allowing himself the luxury, while alone, of playing his games, having fun, asserting himself in that area of playfulness and spontaneity which is so crucial to his character. (In a film such as *8½*, it is particularly important to note when the character is willing and able to assert himself.) On the other hand, his playfulness is subverted by two things: the hall and the same buzzer sound earlier identified with the telephone in the bathroom. The hall is a narrow, dark, tunnel with a mirror at the far end which turns the space back upon the viewer. The somber space captures and accosts Guido, surrounding him on all sides. The buzzer sound has no obvious source; the viewer can only surmise that it is an attempt to subvert the scene with another reminder of the sound stage of a film. This is supported somewhat by the following scene, where the sound is used again and, of course, by the later viewing of the rushes where it is used repeatedly.

10. HOTEL ELEVATOR (INTERIOR). The elevator arrives and Guido steps inside, only to find himself in the presence of the Cardinal and two of his associates. Any desire to laugh at the comic face of the woman who operates the elevator, or at the impish face of the associate who is thumbing pages, is suppressed by the tight, enclosed space of the elevator, and the presence of the Cardinal, a threatening creature from another world. Guido is trapped again. The tiny elevator seems to take forever to reach the lobby floor, where Guido can escape out of the dark box and into some feeling of space and light, away from being trapped and divided between the comic and the solemn, the natural and the formal, the individual and the institutional.

11. SPA HOTEL LOBBY, BY DAY (INTERIOR). The scene is a prime example of the moving camera following Guido relentlessly and holding him within the confines of the frame. As various people confront him with questions and demands, they enter and exit the frame at will

whereas Guido remains, for the most part, trapped by the moving camera. The extremely long takes, with the camera dancing in circles around Guido, help to accentuate the extent to which he is being pursued by people who make demands upon him, pushing for decisions and commitments. As in the tunnel scene and elsewhere in the film the off-screen space is filled with threats and reproach and pressure. Guido avoids making any direct answers or decisions.

The hero's personal crisis is being reflected in and through his occupation as film director. Few hints are offered as to the cause of Guido's crisis. Perhaps he has become aware of his age; perhaps he fears he has lost his creative ability; perhaps he dislikes the film that he has begun making; but nothing is made specific.

As Fellini has said in several interviews it was only after giving his protagonist other occupations that he decided to make him a film director. I suspect that it was difficult to make such a decision. Fellini had to expect that many film viewers would read *8½* as explicit autobiography and never push past that glib observation to understand the film's deeper concern with the spiritual, emotional, physical, and intellectual crisis of a character—an Everyman perhaps—who finds himself paralyzed, moving vertically among various levels of experience without progressing forward; man regressing into childhood, at times seeking to escape responsibility, questioning who he is and what he can do well; man surrounded by people busy about their own concerns and indifferent to his needs and difficulties; man forced to make decisions immediately over matters that are not easily decided.

I can only presume that Fellini chose a film director as the hero because that occupation so perfectly mirrors and focuses such crises. Few occupations force a person to make such decisions, dictate such immediate action, require such a high degree of preplanning and improvization. There is surely no other occupation that requires so much play between a personal vision and the requirements of technology, time, and business. It is also the one profession Fellini knows in the greatest detail and at the deepest levels. At the same time, it should be noted that there is an entire tradition in the independent film (Mekas, Brakhage, Deren) and the commercial film (Truffaut's *Day for Night,* for instance) in which autobiography and the filmmaking process are central concerns.

Guido's crisis is not tragic, of course. It seems integrative and not disintegrative, and its form is therefore comic. When the French actress is introduced (perhaps she has come to play Carla in the film that Guido hopes to make), the soundtrack plays the Tchaikovsky section of the "Concertino alle terme," and this in turn is followed by "To Love Again," a tune based on Chopin's "E Flat Nocturn." Guido is worried by his own aging and yet the prospective fathers are not old enough. A mysterious woman floats by the background and Guido is stunned by her appearance.[17] The lobby of the hotel is a harsh juxtaposition of *art nouveau* and signs of construction. Perhaps the construction is meant to reveal that it is a movie set, much like the buzzer sound which is here repeated when the Cardinal is moving from the elevator toward the door. The dramatic appearance of the producer, from the sky as it were in an open-cage elevator, and Guido's homage also are comic. The godlike producer brings a watch, reminds Guido of the pressure of time, and asks if the director's ideas have matured. Comic though they are, the demands beating at Guido from every side compound his crisis and the scene increases the tension that he must deal with.

12. SPA GROUNDS, BY NIGHT (EXTERIOR). The grounds where the people earlier queued up for mineral water have been transformed into a nightclub. People dance, eat, drink, sit. Throughout the scene there is a medley of tunes from different eras, including a twist, a melody reminiscent of Tommy Dorsey, several others identified on the record as "Cadillac," portions of "Carlotta's Galop," and "E poi." The scene opens with the singing of "Gigolette" and concludes with "L'illusionista," itself a variation on the *8½* theme, and the "Ricordo d'infanzia." The same temporal confusion is evident in the clothes of the characters.

For the most part, until the appearance of Maurice and Maya, the scene seems a recapitulation. Guido is questioned again by the American journalist. The writer, Carini, expresses his same disdain. Several people press Guido for decisions (the French actress and her agent, for instance), but Guido notably avoids direct answers. Carla sits at a nearby table. At the opening of the scene, Guido is wearing a false nose which he has fashioned out of dough or putty. He fingers it, especially as he watches Carla. Later Rossella will call him Pinocchio. The reference is not a strong one, just a slight indication of the character who loves to play, to lie, to fabricate, who is deceived by those he trusts and who, above all, desires to become alive.

The tone of the scene changes dramatically as back lights silhouette the figure of a man and then lights from the front reveal the laughing, white face of Maurice, a magician of sorts. The camera speeds with him as he winds throughout the crowd, waving his wand and fronting for Maya, a mind reader. As the action approaches a peak of rhythm, the wand is seen entering the frame from screen left, the camera follows forward and the wand approaches the table where Gloria is seated. The magician approaches her, promising a demonstration of magnetic force and mental telepathy, but she erupts into a frenzy of rejection. The reasons are not clear. Perhaps she is a sorceress.

The magician moves quickly to another group: Guido and his companions. Guido is hunching down again, toward the ground, as he did once before in the bathroom. Once they get close enough, Maurice and Guido recognize one another. Indeed, they seem to be old friends, companions not only of childhood perhaps but of make-believe and magic, too. A filmmaker is certainly a magician. The two areas, childhood and magic, hold special meaning for Guido at this point in his life and their overlapping will become obvious in the scene that follows. For a moment the camera holds on the two men. In a film, and even in this scene, where the camera moves relentlessly, such settled attention to two people suggests a bond between them. Maya reads Guido's mind and then writes the phrase "Asi Nisi Masa" on the blackboard. The sound of water is heard, perhaps from the springs nearby, and then the "Ricordo d'infanzia" lullaby, as the scene dissolves to the farmhouse of Guido's youth to explain the meaning of "Asi Nisi Masa."

13. A FARMHOUSE, BY NIGHT (INTERIOR). The "Ricordo d'infanzia" music is played and hummed under much of this scene, identifying the place and the music very strongly. The specific actions of this scene are noted in the outline and I have little to add to that list except to point out the episode where Guido runs under the table, fleeing the nurse who wishes to put him in the bath of wine lees, because it suggests Guido's crawling under the table at the press conference later in the film. What is crucial about the scene is its extreme delight in sensuous experience, the unreserved joy of the children in the bath and in the bed, the warm fire, the enveloping sheet, the comforting way in which Guido is put into bed and held by a nurse who cuddles him saying, "dear, sweet boy." All of this happiness is supported by a camera which seems to *float*, winding its way about the warm, en-

closed farmhouse and among the sheets. Indeed, the sheets are a specific motif seen throughout the film, as in the scene in Carla's bedroom, in the steam baths, in the harem, in Claudia's presence under the sheets later, and in several other places, including their similarity to the white clothes at the end of the film and the cloth on the back of La Saraghina's chair. The connotations are not always the same, of course: cleanliness, warmth, purity, shrouds, grave.

Whereas Guido's relationship with his parents as presented at the cemetery was strained and people were separate from one another, here in the farmhouse the opposite effect is crated. The tone of the two scenes is as different as the two spaces in which they occur, one a strange, frightening, open space, and the other a dark, warm womb. Contrasted to the many unpleasant scenes, the camera here does not force itself behind Guido's head, assuming his point of view and reckoning with an intruding world. Rather the camera is pulled back so that the viewer can see the child, Guido, in relation to an environment he finds more comforting and safe. When the camera does move in on Guido's bed, for instance, it is to focus on the nurse as she engulfs him with uncritical love. The reproaching, distant parents and parent types (Luisa, for instance) are absent. The grandmother is there, but she too is uncritical, rambling on about her husband.

This is not to say that the scene is without its disturbing elements. There are dark shadows on the white walls of the farmhouse. The grandmother's face, lit only by a candle, is startling if not, indeed, frightening. The child's discussion of magic manages to mix the worlds of pleasure and unrestrained fear which only a child can feel. The point, of course, is to link these two worlds, magic and pleasure, games and transformation, play and salvation, a twinned joy and terror essentially religious in character. If Guido is living regressively, this is the world that he seeks, one in which the pronouncement of a few ritual words opens the door to the hidden treasure of freedom and play. It is not surprising, therefore, that the magician, Maurice, will signal the transformation at the end of the film.

The farmhouse scene closes with a sequence of still, but mostly moving, shots which caress the farmhouse, floating over candles, oil lamp (seen again in the harem scene and later carried by Claudia as she prepares a table), white walls and space. The way the camera floats strongly recalls Guido in the sky, freed from gravity, and the slight wind noise helps to support this association. The soft sounds of a harp fill the last moments of the scene, as the camera moves about and finally lingers on the warm, crackling fire.

14. SPA HOTEL LOBBY, BY NIGHT (INTERIOR). The scene dissolves slowly back to the lobby of the hotel and the face of the desk clerk who tells Guido that he has had a call from Rome. The change in tone is immediately signalled as the man looks directly into the camera, which has assumed Guido's point of view. The film director asks that the call be put through and then moves away from the desk, walking through the dark, almost empty lobby. At the piano, Mezzabotta is playing a series of tunes for Gloria—a version of the *8½* theme, "E poi," and a part of "Carlotta's Galop." In the quiet evening, the massive statues and other *art nouveau* objects seem very much out of place. As Guido walks through the lobby, he overhears a strained, melodramatic phone conversation being held by the mysterious unknown woman. For a moment, her unrestrained passion makes her even more remote from Guido.

The French actress is in the lobby with her manager, and she accosts Guido, desperately seeking some information about her part and trying to establish a personal relationship with him. While she rambles on, his eye wanders over to Gloria. In a brief close-up of the girl, she gives Guido a provocative gesture of her finger and eyelid. A simple movement, it tells us a great deal about her relationship with men and especially Mario. She leaps to her feet, hits him on the head, and asks him to play "Mystification," a tune which he does not know. It is a role he plays, however. Guido's telephone call comes through and he uses it to escape the French actress, who curses him for his noncommital and indifferent attitude.

In a movement of person and framing of shot which emphasizes the emptiness of the hotel lobby, with its great shadows, the desk clerk moves away from the phone and stands in the middle of the dark lobby as Guido begins to speak. On the phone is his wife, Luisa. Like other events in Guido's life, the telephone conversation is repeatedly interrupted by Luisa's friends. Of special note is the comment by Rossella, who will later refer to herself as Pinocchio's conscience, when she asks Guido if his conscience is bothering him. In any case, in the midst of the confusion, Guido suddenly asks Luisa if she will join him at the spa. The conversation ends irresolutely.

15. A ROOM IN THE SPA HOTEL, EQUIPPED AS A PRODUCTION OF-FICE, BY NIGHT (INTERIOR). The integration of Guido's personal and

professional life is immediately apparent as the viewer discovers that the production office for the film is at Guido's hotel, indeed, right next to his bedroom. The presence of the production office is the first clear indication, unless one considers the buzzer sounds and the exposure of set construction, as in the hotel lobby, that Guido has come to the spa not only for a cure but also to plan and perhaps shoot his film. Indeed, even the "reality" of the cure is suspect, since it could be an episode in the film.[18]

A version of the *8½* theme, "Nell'ufficio produzione di 'Otto e Mezzo' " is heard throughout most of the scene. As in other instances where Guido has to deal directly with aspects of the film, the camera assumes his point of view. He is often absent from the frame, and the people present him with problems and ask for decisions. In a back room, Guido discovers two "nieces," romping in Cesarino's bed. Behind them on the wall is a picture of the spaceship tower, an image of escape and freedom which might be associated with the "nieces." One of the girls remarks that the other has said that Guido is incapable of making a love story. Guido tells her that she is probably right, and the exchange echoes what Claudia will later say, referring to the protagonist in Guido's film, "He doesn't know how to love." To love and to make stories are obviously crucial needs Guido must satisfy. To be creative is to be potent.

16. HALL OF SPA HOTEL, BY NIGHT (INTERIOR). As Guido leaves the production office, he is back in the dark, somber hall, its compressed space accentuated by the mirror at the end which once again turns the space back upon the viewer. There, in that tight, tunnel-like space, Guido runs into Conocchia, an old friend, former film director himself, and now production collaborator. He has been seen several times earlier, as in the tomb with the producer and Guido's father, and also at the night club sequence where he discreetly undermined Guido by telling the producer about some of the film's costs. Later, in the movie house, he will do the same thing. Here in the confines of the hall, however, he berates Guido for not paying more attention to him, for not making better use of him, for turning his back on him. Like the French actress downstairs, Conocchia is asking for a more direct, personal relationship with Guido, something Guido is almost incapable of giving. In the constricted space of the hall, Guido is trapped again and he lashes out at the old man. The "old" reference

is picked up by Conocchia, and the general problem of aging is again stressed.

17. GUIDO'S BEDROOM IN THE SPA HOTEL, BY NIGHT (INTERIOR). Pondering Conocchia's last statement, "You're not the man you used to be," Guido wonders whether or not he has lost his creative talent as an artist, whether or not he ever had any. Ceasing to wait on inspiration, Guido seems to embark on the kind of activity Carini has suggested, trying to determine rationally who and what Claudia is. As he speaks, she enters, and like the ideal mother and nurse, she turns down the bed for Guido, placing his slippers beside the bed. The camera glides with her as she moves in a dance about the room. She emerges from behind the curtains as the nurse at the farmhouse had made her way through sheets. Claudia is there, at least for now, to be Guido's nurse. It is not clear whether the viewer is seeing a scene from the film Guido is making or from one he is contemplating. He is absent from many of these first shots. What is clear is that the talk about Claudia and her actual presence are combined. The confounding of experience is accentuated by the elliptical editing: shots of Claudia are cut together with gaps missing in the action. This device occurs throughout the scene.

But even as Claudia moves about the room, Guido critiques his own attempts at rationalization, saying angrily, "Enough of this symbolism and escapist themes of purity and innocence," thereby negating any easy summaries of what Claudia represents. He slumps down in the bathroom, anointing or wetting his head with a bottle of liquid in a gesture that again relates water and healing. Then, in an abrupt change of pace, as if his inspiration had returned, Guido bursts into statements and movements, the camera moving quickly with him. He suggests who Claudia might be, rushing toward his own notes, and seems for a moment to embark aggressively upon his film. His thoughts are reflected visually as Claudia enters the room and mimics some of the actions Guido suggests. But she turns, places her arms between her legs and breaks into laughter. The role does not suit her. "You're right to laugh," a dejected Guido says, and the camera cuts to him tumbling over on top of a bed littered with photographs. In the contortions of his body, falling backward, and the uneasiness created by the way he mauls the photographs, a simple graphic statement is made, replete with overtones of sexual inadequacy, about the director's separation and alienation from his people—photographic objects. He can't penetrate the flat surface of the photographs; they remain remote, two-dimensional faces.

The tone of the scene changes again. Guido's despair is forgotten for a moment as the viewer watches Claudia return to actions more like those when she first entered the room—the nurse. In a few graceful movements, she plays with a lovely piece of sheer cloth (not so different from those that dance in front of the camera during the harem scene and the one which is attached to the back of La Saraghina's chair on the beach). In the same floating movements, followed by the camera, she moves to Guido, kneeling down to touch, kiss, and caress him. Claudia is now the nurse, caring for him, putting him to bed as in the farmhouse. Then there is a jump cut to Claudia's back, the straps of her slip pulled down over her shoulder. An intimacy is only suggested, however, as Claudia's back remains to the camera. Just as quickly, the camera jumps to Claudia in bed. Guido is absent from these shots. In bed, Claudia has the sheets pulled up to her chin. She caresses the sheets repeating, "I have come to create order, I have come to bring cleanliness," and the camera zooms in on her face.

At such a convincing moment, one which so completely involves the viewer in the immediate experience, it is irrelevant to ask whether the image belongs to a film being contemplated, or being fantasized, or being remembered. More than many other moments in *8½* where dream and dreamer are seen simultaneously, this scene vividly identifies the film Guido is making, the film he is thinking about and planning, the needs of his present and past life, and the film the viewer is seeing. It is all of one fabric and ultimately seamless.

The intertwining of levels of experience is displaced momentarily, however, as another shot of the room, now much more bright, reveals Guido upon the bed, a photograph propped suggestively between his legs. The buzzer sound is heard again; this time it is a telephone. Carla is calling to make her demands upon Guido. She is sick, burning up with fever.

18. CARLA'S BEDROOM, HOTEL TERMINAL, BY NIGHT (INTERIOR). The train whistle is still heard in the background. Carla feverishly rambles on about herself, her husband, her apartment. For a few moments, Guido tries to help, and then he lies down on the bed, his head out of frame, visually estranged from her. The camera cuts to

Guido's face. He is oblivious to Carla's questions, wondering instead what he will say to the Cardinal at their meeting the next day.

19. SPA GROUNDS, BY DAY (EXTERIOR). There is a direct cut to a long, floating shot that trucks in among the eucalyptus trees that surround the outdoor spa area, where earlier the people had queued up for their mineral water. The camera has assumed Guido's point of view again as he is met by the Cardinal's secretary and associate who lead him toward the prelate. One man is on each side of Guido, surrounding him in a manner seen often in the film. Confined by the two men, who stare at him by looking into the camera, Guido is asked about the film he plans to make.

The camera leaves its place among the men and moves in on the Cardinal who is seated on the platform of the spa grounds where the nightclub scene took place, where Guido first saw Claudia, etc.[19] The sound of water is heard nearby. Before Guido can begin his discussion with the Cardinal, the prelate begins to ask personal questions of Guido and then goes off into a speech about the birds whose sobbing sounds are in memory of Diomedes. Like Guido's own father, earlier in the film, the Cardinal does not respond to Guido. The scene would be very comic if it were not for the utter seriousness with which the Cardinal pursues his speech. There is an interesting confusion of experiences here, of course. Presumably, Guido has come to consult about a meeting the film's protagonist will have with a Cardinal in a mud bath area of the underground steam baths. The Cardinal is the same in both scenes, of course, as is Guido. In both scenes, the more important topic of discussion is Guido himself and in both scenes, there is little real attention to Guido's thoughts and questions. The Cardinal remains aloof, a creature belonging to another world. He will be no use to Guido on his spiritual quest.

In the midst of a silence imposed by the Cardinal in order to listen to the birds, Guido looks away and notices a woman coming down the hill nearby. The "Ricordo d'infanzia" music begins and a harsh whistle indicates the abrupt change to another scene.

20. A SCHOOLYARD, BY DAY (EXTERIOR). The back of a man's head blackens the frame. Finally, he turns and the whistle is seen in his mouth. Several boys and a cleric play ball in the background. Outside the schoolyard, a group of boys taunt the child Guido, asking him to join them. The "Ricordo d'infanzia" music fades out and the camera cuts to a high angle shot of Guido. In the foreground is the

statue of another cleric, and it closely resembles the Cardinal seen previously. The shot, of course, juxtaposes the statue and Guido, emphasizing Guido's consternation. But the boy, dressed in his black uniform, sneaks out of the yard anyway and follows the other boys to visit La Saraghina.

21. A BEACH, BY DAY (EXTERIOR). As the boys march across the beach toward La Saraghina's pill box, the camera, as it often does when the scene is pleasant, pulls back to hold on beach, boys, water, and sky. The beach itself is a space repeated often throughout this and other Fellini films. In *8½* it is seen when Guido is being pulled from the sky; it is the site of the tower and also of the final sequences of the film, when Guido's friends and relatives march across the sand to join in the dance around the ring.

La Saraghina's dance is a remarkable event, accomplished by the extraordinary actions of an elephantine creature and the effective use of cinematic devices. A close analysis of the use of the camera and framing reveals the great extent to which they support the feelings of total abandon and freedom, surprise and exhilaration. Many shots, for instance, raise audience expectation by having La Saraghina suddenly dance out of frame, leaving it empty and ready to be filled. The viewer's eye is pulled toward the background, but the harsh, intense beat of the rhumba, and the belief that La Saraghina is somewhere off-screen, heightens the sense that she will suddenly erupt back into view. In such cases, the tension between potential foreground and actual background is evident. In other cases, where the shot is to a new part of the landscape, the viewer is surprised by the unexpected entrance of La Saraghina into frame, her huge body dancing into sight from off-screen. Many of the shots (the entire scene is only sixteen shots long) also involve complex interaction of camera and subject movement—trucking, booming, tilting. There are several dolly movements, too, as when the camera moves in upon the boys and isolates Guido in a close shot. In at least one case, the cut falls upon camera movement. In all the movements of La Saraghina, the camera, the boys, there is a frequent change in the background of each shot and the size of the center of interest. The alternation of interest from foreground to background involves changes in focus, and in one case the racking of focus is quite perceptible.[20]

In Fellini's films, especially here in *8½*, dancing itself has a special importance. In almost every context, dancing, marching, parading, processions are associated with pleasure, ecstasy, reunion, and resurrection of spirit. For instance, in *8½*, there is not only La Saraghina's joyful rhumba, but also Mario and Gloria's twist. When Guido and Luisa meet on the spa street, the first thing they do is to go and dance, remarking that it's been over a year since they have danced. The film's affirmative finale is a dance around the circus ring. In the harem, Jacqueline Bonbon's decisive fault is that she can no longer dance. When Guido imagines that Carla and Luisa are friends, they are seen dancing.

Several aspects of La Saraghina's dance are exaggerated and even broadly comic. The accordion noise is pushed to the extreme; at one point, La Saraghina is obviously speaking and her words are drowned out by the sound of the instrument which emanates from some unknown source. The action is speeded up when Guido is chased and caught by the priests. Without being too obvious, the film is asking that the viewer experience the events not realistically but as remembered and felt by Guido, a common practice throughout *8½*.

22. SCHOOL, BY DAY (INTERIOR). Dragged away from the beach by the two priests, who lead Guido directly into the camera, the young boy is now taken back to the school for punishment. The vigorous rhumba beat is replaced by the stiff, mechanical ringing of a hand bell or some similar instrument. Indeed, one of the formal strategies of this scene, contrasting La Saraghina's dance, is to cut quite mechanically, motivated almost entirely by the speeches. Similarly, the compositions of the people in the frame and the arrangement of people in the room are formal, austere, with people almost evenly spaced in their distance from one another. Thus, the psychological distance between Guido and the other people, particularly his mother, is emphasized. There is almost no human contact. The people, including his mother, keep him at a distance, reproaching him with biting speeches of "Shame, mortal shame!"

The general attitude about the clerics is portrayed almost immediately when the moving camera, trucking past large portraits, stops and zooms in on a living face almost as lifeless as the paintings. The moment of ambiguity and surprise is as much a comment upon the nature of the priests as is the choice of women to play the roles. This attitude is supported by the indifferent reproachment of the priests, their downcast faces, their pointed fingers. Their feelings about Guido and his action are also supported by the camera, as it moves from

face to face, often zooming rapidly in upon a face just as it pronounces some condemning remark, thereby making the remark even
more harsh. The scene also contains two other strategies already
identified as means of accosting Guido. When Guido is led in and
taken out, he is surrounded on both sides by the accusing teachers.
Moreover, several times in the scene, the father superior (or school
president) and the others look directly toward the camera because it
has assumed Guido's point of view. This use of the camera is particularly evident when one of the clerics points an accusing finger
directly at the lens, that is, at Guido.

The imposition of guilt, the rejection of Guido, even by his
mother, the harsh black and white contrasts, the camera that moves
quickly to right or left to reveal an off-screen space filled with a
judgmental person, the portrait of a saintly child behind the accusing
mother, the lack of human contact, the mechanical camera work and
cutting—all these strategies have appeared before in the film. But
the scene turns upside down any generalizations the viewer might
have been making about the use of space. Here, the context and
cinematic strategies create the same feelings of guilt and suffocation
and entrapment that have been associated with small, dark, tunnel
spaces. Carla's bedroom was a similar inversion of such spatial associations. Vacancy comes in all sizes.

23. SCHOOL CLASSROOM, BY DAY (INTERIOR). The camera pans
with one boy as he runs from a boisterous group to slap someone
else. This camera movement also picks up, in the background, Guido
entering screen right. Separated from his classmates, he wears a sign,
"Shame," on his back.

24. SCHOOL LUNCHROOM, BY DAY (INTERIOR). Guido is being
further humiliated and punished as dried peas, or some kind of kernels, are poured into a bowl and then emptied onto the floor where he
is forced to kneel upon them. While a voice drones on about the
pious Jesuit boy saint, Aloysius Gonzaga, who would run from
women, a cleric slaps Guido to keep him kneeling upon the hard
kernels. A swift zoom in to the person who slaps Guido accentuates
the discrepancy between the pious words and the pitiless treatment
of Guido. The cleric who slaps Guido sanctimoniously clasps his
hands and exits screen right. Guido is left alone in the middle of the
room, isolated, punished, guilty.

25. CHURCH/SCHOOL, BY DAY (INTERIOR). The scene probably

takes place in the chapel of the school, although there are no clear visual clues. The scene opens with a shot of something encased in glass, and the child Guido is seen behind the case. Bells are heard in the background. Guido suddenly turns and runs off screen right. The camera moves part of the way with him and then stops to reveal that the figure in the case is the mummified body of someone, perhaps a saint, perhaps an ordinary woman. Whereas the pious Aloysius (Luigi) fled from women, Guido flees the grotesque saint. The suffocating enclosure of the mummified body is similar to other spaces in the film—Guido's car in the tunnel, the father's tomb, the Fakir's box. Moreover, the child Guido is fleeing something that probably bothers the man Guido, the sight of aging and death. At least, La Saraghina's "shameful" dance represented life.

26. CHURCH/SCHOOL, BY DAY (INTERIOR). In another part of the school's chapel, perhaps, a group of confessionals stand strange, dark, and austere against the bright, white walls. The camera moves forward, pushing the viewer inside the dark, foreboding space, once again into oppressive enclosure. The curtain is drawn, the door slid back, and the priest reviles Guido again, telling him that La Saraghina is the devil. The usual formalities of the confession are deleted in order to stress this one statement and to emphasize Guido's entrapment, his estrangement from the priest.

Guido leaves the confessional and walks toward the camera, placed high to encompass the entire space. In the background, the priest exits. In the foreground, there is a statue of what appears to be the Virgin Mother. The face resembles that of the unknown, mysterious woman, Caterina Boratto, seen earlier in the hotel lobby. The "Ricordo d'infanzia" music is heard in the background of the soundtrack. Guido kneels before the statue. The camera moves up to hold on the face of the statue and then there is a long, slow dissolve from the face to La Saraghina's pill box.

27. BEACH, BY DAY (EXTERIOR). The "Ricordo d'infanzia" music continues, eventually to be replaced by the rhumba tune, this time hummed by La Saraghina more in the rhythm of a lullaby. The slow dissolve from statue to pill box, in the overall context of the film, shows how Guido's crisis is involved with the attraction and repulsion of certain kinds of women. Guido approaches La Saraghina's pill box, in spite of all the punishment he has received because of her. Even if she is the devil, he is attracted to her. La Saraghina sits quietly in a

chair beside the sea, humming. Attached to the back of her chair is a white cloth which blows in the wind, reminding us ever so slightly of the white sheets and clothes that appear elsewhere in the film. Guido is pulled toward her. The camera trucks screen right with him as he walks along the beach, carrying him along toward the woman. Just as he kneeled before the religious statue, he now comes and kneels before La Saraghina. She looks back at Guido and says, in a simple and inviting voice, "Ciao." Still kneeling, the boy waves his hat at her. Despite the excesses of the rhumba, the pronouncements of the clerics, La Saraghina now seems a beautiful, uncritical, accepting creature.

28. SPA HOTEL DINING ROOM, BY DAY (INTERIOR). The "Ricordo d'infanzia" music carries over a long dissolve from La Saraghina to the Cardinal, sitting down with his associates at a table in the dining room. In previous scenes, he has seemed so remote that it is startling to hear him tell a joke. A tension is created between this background scene and the foreground, where Guido and Carini are seated. The latter, almost as if he is referring to the scenes the viewer has just seen, is berating Guido, "But these are only childhood memories; they mean nothing for the film." Guido gets up to leave, but Carini follows. As they exit screen left, they pull into frame a woman who is singing. The camera has assumed Guido's point of view again, emphasizing his distance from the Cardinal and Carini. The scene serves as a slight caesura between the memories of La Saraghina and the frenzy of the scene which follows.

29. UNDERGROUND STEAM BATHS, BY DAY (INTERIOR). The music of the woman singing in the dining room segues into a brisk beat being played by a combo in a new environment: the entrance to the underground baths of the spa. This "Discesa al fanghi" music, which includes portions of "Carlotta's Galop" and "Cimitero" will continue throughout the scene. It is particularly impressive as it provides the background and the rhythm for the descent of a great many people down the stairs.

The presence of people and things off-screen is emphasized as, early in the scene, a woman's face emerges from below the frame line. The camera follows her as she speaks to her doctor, then moves to join the many people swathed in sheets as they move down the steps to the steam rooms. This is innately a very funny scene, but the people shown are utterly serious. They wrap themselves willingly in their shrouds and allow themselves to be sent down into the Inferno or Purgatory. Herded around by muscular men stripped to the waist, called by numbers over the loudspeakers, stepping along to the music, perspiring profusely, the people accept it all, willingly enduring the indignity as well as the heat and steam. As Guido sits down on one of the benches, he realizes he is next to Mezzabotta who, almost overcome by the heat, does not open his eyes or answer when Guido speaks to him. It is indeed a world of isolation.

The close shot of Mario's face serves as a transition into another mode of experience. The camera cuts back to a wide shot of the steam room just as a voice, resembling that of the stewardess heard later in the harem, announces that the Cardinal will now see Guido. It is, of course, difficult to know what to make of this event. Is the viewer suddenly being transported to the film Guido was going to make or is making? It was just such a meeting that he was going to discuss in that abortive meeting with the Cardinal. The answer is deliberately left unclear. The "Cimitero" section of the "Discesa al fanghi" music is now evident.

As the quality of the sound changes, and as the camera pulls back to a wider view of the steam bath area, there follows a sudden reverse angle in which a rapidly moving camera is identified with Guido, assuming his point of view and his movements, as he travels through the corridors toward his meeting with the Cardinal. Various people move into the frame (Guido's viewpoint), intruding themselves upon Guido from that ever present off-screen space, handing him clothes to put on, asking him for favors of the Cardinal—a Mexican divorce, the success of the film. The sensuous flow of the camera is subverted by the threatening way in which people so blithely enter the frame from off-screen, stare directly into the camera, and make demands upon Guido. Pace, the producer, is particularly comic in his appearance and his pleas.

Finally, the camera angle reverses momentarily and Guido is seen in the distance, now dressed in his black suit, walking away down one of the corridors in the baths. Just as quickly, however, the camera again assumes his point of view and one of the Cardinal's associates approaches to say that Guido only has five minutes. Like a voyeur, the camera approaches a small window which opens, as if by magic, so that Guido (the camera viewpoint) can peer into the most private place where the Cardinal is having his steam and mud bath. It is an outsider's view. The same feeling of alienation is created and amplified by the Cardinal, separated from Guido and the viewer by white sheets. When Guido says, "I'm not happy," the Cardinal responds with a rehearsed, indifferent speech. As the Cardinal speaks of the City of God, the foreground is filled with hands squeezing mud, an ironic counterpoint to the prelate's words. Guido's questions are serious and the Cardinal's speech is ethereal. The scene is blatantly comic.

Most striking about the scene is Guido's absence from it, and this, as we have noted, is a strategy used frequently in *8½*. From the very moment when he asks about his own happiness, Guido is not seen. He is absent as the camera moves through the window into the Cardinal's sacred quarters, peers upon the Cardinal, or at least what can be seen of him behind the sheets and the steam, and then retreats out the same window as it closes decisively after the backward moving camera. The choice which the Cardinal demands, between the City of God and the City of the Devil, has nothing directly to do with Guido as an individual human being. It is a choice posed in the abstract, and the answer belongs to some other world, not the one to which Guido belongs.

30. STREET NEAR SPA HOTEL, BY NIGHT (EXTERIOR). The song "Blue Moon" is heard even as the tiny door closes on the Cardinal's room in the previous scene. Now, as the present scene appears, the source of the music is seen to be a woman playing a violin. The night coolness has brought a number of people out to walk the streets of the spa or thermal resort. The streets are lined with shops containing auctions, exhibitions, and other tourist attractions. A Fakir is enclosed within a glass case. His barker stands outside with a microphone, announcing that the Fakir has broken all endurance records for remaining within such an enclosure. It is a spatial and spiritual condition echoed throughout the film. Along these streets, with the strains of "Blue Moon" in the background, Guido walks. The camera picks him up just as he sees his wife, Luisa, whereupon he resorts to biting his nails, a nervous habit he displays several times in the film. Guido hesitates for a moment, following her. Finally it is Luisa who notices her husband. When they meet it is in front of a store window that contains a seascape. In the context of Fellini's films, where there is such obsession with the sea and water as places where salvation is

often found, such a manufactured seascape background is a gentle joke.

31. OUTDOOR CAFE NEAR THE SPA HOTEL, BY NIGHT (EXTERIOR). Almost as quickly as Guido and Luisa have met, they are seen together in another place, dancing. They move to the "Nostalgic Swing," itself a variation of the *8½* theme and containing elements of "Carlotta's Galop" and other music in the film. In the context of other dancing in the film, it is especially important when they remark that they haven't danced together in a year. And when Guido remarks that Luisa feels "light," it is difficult to disassociate that remark from the frequent allusions to floating and freedom found in *8½;* the remark and the dancing seem to suggest the possibility of happiness for the couple. Even the presence of Enrico, an admirer of Luisa's, is more playful than threatening. A man approaches the producer and asks him to produce his script about nuclear disarmament. There are several playful references to Guido's harem, remarks which will of course have further meaning later in the film. The producer refuses to touch Rossella's hand because she might read his mind through his fingertip. As offhanded as the remark may seem, it fits into that larger pattern of magic and mysticism pervading the film. Later Guido will ask Rossella to ask the spirits for guidance. For the most part, however, the statements all seem rather innocent and natural at the moment, and the scene is light and humorous, until Pace invites everyone, including Luisa, her sister, and her friends to visit the tower. As Luisa is moving toward the car, something happens. This turn of events is dramatically signalled by the pan of the camera which suddenly reveals in the foreground an aged, strained face, made frightening by its abrupt appearance from off-screen. Luisa gets into the front seat of the car, refusing to ride with Guido. Not until the next day will the viewer learn that her sudden change in attitude is caused by seeing Carla on the spa street. Quickly, the dancing and all it implies have stopped.

32. SPACESHIP TOWER, BY NIGHT (EXTERIOR). A dissolve changes the scene from the cars on the spa street to the tower on the beach. A lantern swings in the foreground. Eerie music emphasizes the strangeness of the huge metal and concrete scaffolding which, in Guido's proposed film, is to be the launching site for a spaceship that will enable the people of the earth to escape to another planet. Some of

the painted glass which will help to create this illusion is noted by the people as they arrive, helping to call attention to the filmmaking process again.

Except for the nighttime sight of the spaceship tower, and its obvious identification with earlier ideas of escape and flying, with objects bizarre and surreal, most of the scene revolves around the dialogue between Guido and Rossella, both of whom remain on the ground while Luisa, Enrico, the producer, and other members of the entourage walk up into the tower. The conversation between Rossella and Guido, clothed in the night shadows, is his first explicit statement about his film. One part of the conversation is a confession on Guido's part. He wanted to make an honest film, one which would bury everything dead in people, one in which he said something. Now he has nothing to say, yet he must say it anyway.[21] The stupid tower is built, a symbol of something dishonest and untruthful. He can't bring himself to use it or order its destruction. He turns again to the world of magic. Guido needs a miracle, and he wishes that Rossella's spirits would help him. She relays a message from her spirit world: "You're free, but you have to choose; and there isn't much time left." To the confused man who has just revealed the extent of his paralysis and despair, Rossella adds, "you must hurry." The scene ends on this frustating note.[22]

33. GUIDO'S HOTEL BEDROOM, BY NIGHT (INTERIOR). Guido is back in his bed, biting his fingernails nervously. Hearing footsteps, he quickly turns off the light and pretends to be sleeping as Luisa enters. She makes a telephone call that seems an attempt to be unfaithful, but it is abortive. Indeed, as she quickly and laughingly says to Guido, it is impossible for her to pursue his kind of deceit and falsehood. The couple, surrounded by the shadows of the room, engage in a fierce argument, each accusing the other of making impossible and un-reasonable demands. The notion of his falsehood (Pinocchio) is central to Luisa's complaints, and no doubt his attitude toward Luisa was most clearly revealed when, at the cemetery, Luisa replaced his mother in the embrace. Both women are distant, critical, demanding. Just as the mother, at the school, kept Guido at arm's length, Luisa now rejects him by turning in bed, her back to his face. Guido, in his own bed, does the same. The camera, having pulled back to a wide view of the room, reveals the completeness of their separation, and the scene fades to black, making even more ominous the argument.

34. OUTDOOR CAFE NEAR THE SPA HOTEL, BY DAY (EXTERIOR). A fade-in reveals a bright, glaring day, as Guido, Rossella, and Luisa are seated outdoors. Its white curtains blowing in the wind, a horse-drawn carriage approaches to the brisk music of "Carlotta's Galop." In her extravagant dress, Carla becomes even more comic as she realizes, having disembarked from the carriage, that she is but a few feet from Luisa and Guido. She awkwardly tries to step out of sight somehow, but it is impossible, and she goes nonchalantly to a table. The camera refuses to show all four parties in the same frame.

Luisa informs Guido that she had seen Carla the night before. Guido lies with an absolutely straight face, even to the point of substantiating his own ridiculous position by saying, "Would I go with anyone who dressed like that?" Luisa, further angered by Guido's obstinate lying, becomes even more vindictive, labeling Carla a cow. Although the viewer knows that Guido is not telling the truth, Luisa has scant evidence, except Carla's presence. In her somewhat unwarranted anger, the viewer gets a glimpse of the kind of jealousy and moral judgments with which Guido has had to live.

The tone of the scene changes dramatically as Guido slouches down in his chair, puts on his sunglasses, touches his Pinocchio nose, and the music becomes more carefree and humorous. The camera then reverses angle and dollies in on Carla, who is singing with great accomplishment. That the mode of experience has somehow changed is quickly confirmed as Luisa enters the frame, compliments Carla, and begins to dance with her. In this ritual of friendship and union they soon pass Guido, who claps approvingly, his feet propped upon the table. The camera has now brought all three people together in the same frame; they are to appear as friends. The dreamer and the dream are united again in the same image. Two disparate aspects of Guido's life are united, dancing together to a variation of the *8½* theme. The change has happened quickly, and viewers are left to confront the immediate experience and to resolve for themselves any discordant aspects.

35. THE FARMHOUSE (INTERIOR). The "L'Harem" music is as much a concatenation of various tunes heard throughout *8½* as the harem itself is a mixture of all the women in Guido's life. The farmhouse of Guido's remembered youth has now been transformed into the fantasy of his adulthood, a true harem in which all the women of his life dwell together in happiness and accord. Curiously, there are

few overtones of sexuality in the harem, except when once or twice Guido's sexual ability is minimized. But there is little discord. Luisa has helped to bring that about by becoming the domestic for the harem, washing, cooking, scrubbing the floors. And when there are moments of discord, as when Jacqueline Bonbon refuses to obey the house rule and retire upstairs, the situation does not get out of control. In most of the worlds that Guido imagines, he is able to act decisively. The harem is not just a place where there is peace and order, a place where Guido can come in out of the cold snowstorm outside; it is also a place where, when necessary, he is able to perform, to choose, to decide. In this respect, it resembles the way in which Guido would like to act, the way in which he directs the dance around the circus ring at the end of the film.

As Guido enters and distributes gifts, the camera often assumes his point of view. People move in and out of frame but this off-screen space is not threatening, just present, as the women enter and exit with their greetings, picking up their gifts. Eventually, the camera moves back to a wider shot to watch the women care for Guido. In a manner reminiscent of the way he was cared for and bathed in the wine lees at the farmhouse, the women undress him, put him into the bath, dry him off, and, finally, wrap him like a baby in white sheets and carry him off as in a cradle. Only Claudia and Guido's mother are conspicuous by their absence. Everyone is there to please and serve him, but there is no hint of erotic sexuality. Even Rossella is present, ready to add her own insight by saying that she is present to serve as Pinocchio's nagging conscience.

Almost invariably in *8½*, as I have pointed out, a gratuitous camera movement (unmotivated by any movement in the frame) has been associated with some unpleasant experience. The same strategy is now used in the harem scene, as the camera trucks screen right in order to reveal something previously off-screen. As the camera stops, looking down a flight of steps, Jacqueline Bonbon climbs up. A section of the "Cimitero" is heard (another place where the same camera movement was used) as Jacqueline announces, replete in her dancer's feathery costume, that despite house rules she will not retire upstairs. No matter about her age; that doesn't matter. The "Rivolta nell'Harem" (Wagner's *Ride of the Valkyries*) music begins to build as Jacqueline protests and her protests fire up the anger of the other women. The camera seeks out crying, distraught faces, one by one, then cuts from one angry woman to another. Each pan, each cut, reveals the space around Guido (the camera has more or less assumed his point of view for a moment) to be threatening again. Finally, as the cries and the music and the accusations and La Saraghina's growl reach a peak, Guido stands up, grabs his whip, and proceeds to bring his wild animals into line, cracking the tip over dresses, bottoms and hairpieces. Earlier he had said that the French actress resembled a snail; now he quickly removes the offending peaks of her hair-do. The women scurry about the room. Large shadows from the moving lanterns are obvious on the white walls. Once again Guido is in command. The gratuitous camera movements of the revolt, the rapid cutting of the whip lashing, have now been replaced by wider shots of the space. Jacqueline is sent upstairs. In one last gesture of magnanimity, she is allowed to dance. But "La ballerina pensionata (Ça c'est Paris)" is abortive. Her costume and pearls drop everywhere. She can no longer dance; she is finished.

After Jacqueline is sent upstairs Guido gives a speech to the contrite women, who are concerned that they may have hurt his feelings. Carla plucks professionally on the harp as the camera continues to pull back to a wider, more comfortable shot, finally revealing Luisa involved in all her domestic chores—washing, scrubbing floors. For a few moments she carries the same oil lamp that was seen in the farmhouse earlier, in Guido's childhood, and which Claudia will carry later. The scene is a fantasy of some sort—remembered, imagined, dreamed, created for the cinema. The presence of the cinema is obvious when Luisa kneels down, and a small spotlight conveniently comes on to light the floor she is scrubbing. It is as improbable on one level as the speech Luisa delivers is unlikely on another level. She talks about how she finally understands that this is the way it is supposed to be—the harem, the domestic chores, everything. Now they can have a happy marriage.

The harem scene is a lived piece; that is, at the moment of happening, the viewer is totally caught up in the experience. This conscription of belief is achieved in several ways, notably in the many small details of action and character—Gloria's positive response to the whip, for instance. In addition, as in La Saraghina's dance, the camera and the cutting force the viewer to be carried along, however unwillingly. When the revolt is building, a camera movement captures the pent-up frenzy of the women: it pans screen right to one woman,

then back screen left to another woman, then back screen right to
follow-focus on La Saraghina screen right into a close-up. Here, as
elsewhere, the camera refuses to release the viewer, to allow for time
to step back and contemplate some of the more comic aspects of the
sequence.

36. MOTION PICTURE THEATER, BY NIGHT (INTERIOR). An ex-
ceptionally long dissolve links Luisa, on her knees scrubbing the floor,
to a close shot of Guido's face, as if reacting (the script calls for an
intervening scene, however) to her by saying, "Please be patient a
little bit longer with me, Luisa." As soon as Guido has made his plea,
the camera pulls back to reveal a large motion picture theater. A
small group (Luisa and her friends, Carini, members of the production staff, Guido, the producer) is assembling to watch some screen
tests for the proposed film. Carini quotes sarcastically from Stendhal
about the solitary ego, attempting further to criticize Guido, but with
a flick of his wrist Guido commands that Carini be hanged. Which
he promptly is. Without any adjustment for a change in kind of experience, what Guido wishes comes true on the screen. The man and
what he wishes exist side by side in time and space. Only a variation
of the *8½* theme, presented as the hanging takes place, suggests that
the event belongs to some other area of experience and is not truly
happening at the moment.

A great deal of pressure is again being exerted upon Guido to
decide, to pick one actor or actress over another. But he cannot decide, no matter how adamant the producer becomes.

The presentation of the screen tests is an even more heightened
example of the overlapping of modes of experience and Guido's re-
lated confusion. This is heightened by the viewer's involvement when
the theater lights go down and the screen in the film becomes identified
with the screen the viewer himself is watching. The characters in the
rushes, or screen tests, are ones the viewer has become acquainted
with: Luisa, La Saraghina, Carla. Only now those familiar characters
have slightly different faces, voices, and movements. It is disorienting to viewers, who thus are made to feel something like Guido's own
confusion. The film director is supposed to choose between these
variations on the same characters. The decision-making process is
magnified, its pressures further heightened. Guido truly must decide.
But the characters seem so alike and they pass by so quickly.

There is hardly another scene in *8½* which makes so vivid Guido's paralysis, confusion, inability, and communicates these experiences to the viewer so well. A great deal of this success is due to the use of the cinematic processes themselves to implode the film upon itself, requiring that the viewer reflect even more consciously upon the medium and the confusion between the medium and the illusion it can create.

Even more apparent in the present scene is that Guido's confusion, if confusion it be, is really that of the person who assimilates and identifies spectacle (the film he is making, planning, thinking about, has made) and life (what he does when he is not filming or thinking about filming or thinking about what he has filmed). For Guido, the distinction between what his imagination creates and the rest of experience is often meaningless. Indeed, for him, everything is imagined, in the sense that his imagination is the constitutive power that creates his world.

The identification of spectacle and life is clearly seen throughout the film but particularly here. The close connection between Guido and the characters on his movie screen is exemplified, for instance, in the exchanges of dialogue which directly relate screen characters and people in the auditorium.[23] The dialogue sometimes moves from screen to auditorium, from Guido as director of the screen tests, to Guido sitting in the auditorium, to the actress trying out for the role of Luisa, to Luisa sitting in the auditorium. The flow of dialogue ties together spectacle and life (to oversimplify) as if they were all of one fabric. The interchange, of course, also points up the confusion concerning Guido's veracity. After so many instances in which spectacle, in whatever form, and life are undifferentiated, the nature of lying is itself questioned.

The distinction between truth and falsehood is very real for Luisa, however, and after biting her nails through the screen tests she finally gets up and leaves. The screen tests are too embarrassing, the wife on the screen is too much like her, everything is too much a reflection of what Guido thinks. And you lie, Luisa says, in a confrontation in a hall outside the theater; you don't know the difference between truth and falsehood. Telling him to go to hell, she stomps out with a frightening finality. The camera, having kept them separated in the hall, now allows her to exit frame.

Guido returns to the dark movie theater even more depressed. On the screen he is aggressive, giving orders, making demands, urging the people on, but sitting in the auditorium he is paralyzed. The producer almost demands that he choose, but Guido cannot.

The cinematic building of the crisis for Guido as man, husband, director, has been done not only by means of a complex interplay of screen tests and action in the theater, but also by a well orchestrated use of sound, editing, and camera movement. The different characters trying out for the same role have been presented elliptically, the jump cuts between persons making even more confusing their presence. The buzzer sound, heard several times previously, is now heard repeatedly and is definitely identified with a motion picture stage. As this crescendo is about to peak, as the producer is about to decide for Guido, another interruption takes him off the hook. In what appears at first to be a threatening gesture, two men come up on either side of Guido. But it is to tell him that Claudia has arrived. Guido is elated and rushes over to meet her. Although nothing has been said explicitly in the film, there is some suggestion that the actress is a figure he has been desperately waiting for and that she will somehow solve his problems. They quickly leave the theater and drive away in her car. "Blue Moon" can be heard softly in the background.

37. AN OLD PIAZZA OR STREET, BY NIGHT (EXTERIOR). Guido is moving again. His heart beats like a schoolboy's, he says. Claudia seems to promise so much for him. He unloads upon her all, or almost all, of his serious thoughts about himself and the film. Is she capable of throwing away everything in order to give herself to one thing? She does not respond directly, asking for directions to drive. Then she throws the question back on him. No, Guido answers. There are springs nearby (the idea of water and healing again), and he asks her to pull off. They pull into a narrow old street, resembling a piazza with all the houses and doors facing the center.

38. STREET/PIAZZA, BY NIGHT (EXTERIOR). Claudia has not immediately fulfilled Guido's expectations. As the car stops, the camera moves slowly toward the people in the car, cuts, and slowly booms up one of the exterior walls of a house along the ancient street. The movement stops as it reveals an open window where Claudia, dressed in white, is picking up the same oil lamp seen twice earlier. She moves in that ethereal manner seen before. The shot cuts to a wider view of the street as she is setting a table in the middle of the street. She places the lamp upon the table and moves in a semicircle back and forth

around the back of the table. Her gentle, disembodied movement is as important as the action she performs as nurse and housekeeper.

Again, the dream or vision or fantasy or film has taken place in the same spot as those who imagine it. Bergman's *Wild Strawberries* has an earlier use of such a strategy, when Borg walks into his own childhood.[24] The confusion of modes of experience is accentuated when Claudia says Guido looks very funny, made up to look like an older man and dressed in black clothes. The viewer is still watching a film within a film. The effect of such mixtures is startling, calling attention to the artificial illusion of the cinema and the way that space articulates time and modes of experience. In *8½*, the viewer is seldom allowed to lose sight of the fact that it is a film he is watching. It is a self-reflexive experience. Guido oscillates in space. It is his movement into and out of himself, toward and away from his fate, backward and forward in time, from side to side in fantasy, that articulates the film. *8½* is a film by a filmmaker making a film about a filmmaker trying to make a film about himself as a man and as a filmmaker.[25]

The camera, having watched Claudia in close-up move gently back and forth around the table, now cuts to a shot looking over the hood of the car at the two people inside. They seem to have shared the vision, for Claudia asks, "Then what happens?" They get out of the car, stepping into the middle of the sixteenth-century street, its plaster walls flaking. At times the film has suggested that Guido discovers something by moving back in time. Now he and Claudia stand in the middle of a street lined with ancient, decaying buildings which surround them on both sides.[26]

Claudia, however, is revealed not to be any of the things Guido had dreamed or imagined. The camera, and its framing, set them apart spatially. She is on one side of the street and he on the other. They are just as far apart in their thinking. She doesn't like the place, it doesn't seem real. He likes it enormously. He needs to fly, to soar. She hunches down in a doorway, her black boa wings clipped and motionless, the feathers scattered on the street. Friendly and gentle as the conversation might be, it is devastating, a renunciation of everything that has gone before. The person Guido has been waiting for has come and almost immediately he rejects her. Guido, the man who saw many of his problems as an oscillation between different kinds of women, now rejects Claudia, come in the flesh, saying that no woman can save a man. And she repeatedly replies, referring as much to him as to the hero of the proposed film, "He doesn't know how to love." The camera cuts back and forth from person to person, emphasizing their separation and their growing awareness. Claudia, listening to Guido talk, realizes that he has fooled her. The image of Pinocchio again. You lied to me, she says, there is no part for me in the film. Guido's reply, given in the quiet, ancient street, is perhaps the most honest thing he has said thus far in the film, or so he imagines. There is no part, not even a film. A pause, a moment of respite, and Guido is caught up in his own despair. To Claudia he has said what he dared not say to anyone else.

Then, suddenly, Claudia's face goes stark white in the glare of an automobile light. The music erupts into a quickened pace, a variation of the *8½* theme that shortly becomes "La conferenza stampa del regista," and the men in the swiftly passing automobiles announce that the producer has started the film himself, in his own way. There is to be a cocktail party and news conference at the spaceship tower the next day.

39. SPACESHIP TOWER PRESS CONFERENCE AND COCKTAIL PARTY, BY DAY (EXTERIOR). For analysis, the point where Guido seems to commit suicide will be used to divide the present beach scene from the one that follows.

8½ began with a scene of cars jammed into a tunnel. The present scene opens with a similar view, but this time the cars are moving— away from the viewer and toward the tower in the distance. The interim scenes seem like a very long parenthesis. The period of stalling and hesitation seems superficially to be over, despite Guido. The director's reluctance is very obvious. He has to be led, sometimes dragged, by his two production assistants toward the cocktail party and press conference. As elsewhere in the film, he is caught between two men. He tries repeatedly to get away but they continue to force him toward the tower. Guido's resistance is counterpointed by the frenzied beat of "La conferenza stampa del regista," a compilation of several pieces of music already used in the film and containing a variation of the *8½* theme.

The press conference scene is a culmination of all the pressures placed upon Guido and a recapitulation of all the cinematic strategies used to reveal them and his response. A swarm of people accost, accuse, and reproach him. Statements and decisions are demanded.

The press is vicious, rapidly asking unanswerable questions and denouncing him. The producer threatens him with ruin if he does not speak about the film. Guido is surrounded on all sides by a disdainful Carini, a weeping Conocchia, intruding photographers, and even Luisa who, appearing in her wedding gown, asks Guido if he will ever truly marry her. The incongruity of her dress and question is not out of place in such a frenetic atmosphere. Guido keeps trying to escape, either by leaving or by refusing to answer. He calls out for Claudia, for the spirits of Rossella.

The extreme pressure being exerted upon Guido is articulated not only in a barrage of questions and statements, themselves absurd, but is reinforced and also expressed by cinematic strategies—the frantic and complex movement of camera and people, the rapid and harsh cutting, the displacement of objects in the frame, the brisk musical tempo. Almost every shot involves quick and extensive trucking, dollying, and booming movements of the camera coupled with complex choreography of moving people, their bodies, hands, faces. The viewer is drawn to some sight in the background and then, suddenly, the frame is filled with something in the foreground. Sometimes the emphasis is reversed. This spatial displacement is often accomplished by camera movement, sometimes by movement of people and objects. In all cases, there is a frenetic articulation not only between foreground and background but also between on-screen and off-screen space. Another strategy used to accentuate the delirium is frequent change in screen direction—of the camera movement, of people in the frame. Moreover, there are many cuts unmotivated by the action: the camera suddenly moves in an unexpected direction or cuts to another part of the scene disconnected from that just shown. This disorientation of the viewer helps to accelerate the frenetic pace and to emphasize Guido's own confusion.

The pace is so rapid, the movement so frequent, the disorienting and disquieting elements so persistent, that the scene is frightening, the viewer overwhelmed by the feeling of being swept along unwillingly through some inexorable movement which nothing can stop. The feeling of fear is again reinforced by having the camera often assume Guido's point of view; at other times, perhaps in an even more frightening way, people act threateningly toward the camera view even when it is physically impossible for the camera to represent Guido's point of view. The harassment and antagonism directed at the camera are directed at the viewer. He is trapped. The film director is trapped. The mirror top to the long table helps to increase the number of accusing faces which surround Guido and press in upon him.

When the scene has nearly reached its frenzied peak, Agostino tells Guido that he has put a gun in his pocket and the film director crawls under the table, trying to evade the people just as he tried playfully to evade the nurse at the farmhouse. He pulls the gun out of his pocket while voices search him out. There is a cut to a scene of Guido's mother, on the beach. She turns and the camera rushes backward even as she cries out to Guido, asking him where he is running to. Before the backward movement of the camera has stopped, there is the sound of a gunshot. Then Guido is seen again, slumping down to the floor under the table. An ellipsis in the action keeps the viewer from actually seeing Guido shoot himself, although that action is implied.

The ellipsis seems to me a deliberate way of helping the viewer to cope. In the present scene, the overall impression is made clear by the context, the elliptical cutting, the cutaway to the mother, the camera's flight from the mother. *8½* has often made use of immediate visual analogies (was Carini hanged in the motion picture theater?) and the representation of Guido's suicide is no exception. Pushed to the extreme, Guido is withdrawing, or thinking of escaping, or wishing to liberate himself. And these desires are most directly expressed by an image of him committing suicide. He wishes to run away— from mother, from film, from press conference, from sex, from accusations, from himself—and this pain and anguish is expressed in the image of suicide. The film has sufficiently prepared the viewer for such an event; that is, for a moment when a wish is communicated in the same mode as any other level of experience.

40. SPACESHIP TOWER ON THE BEACH, BY DAY AND NIGHT (EXTERIOR). The metaphoric representations at the press conference seem to have had some actual counterpart, for Guido and Carini are now watching the dismantling of the tower. The implication is that the picture has been halted. Carini continues to drone on about the wisdom of Guido's decision, but Guido himself is absorbed in doubts and further self-analysis. In the midst of this situation, the film's epiphany takes place. And this final scene must be dealt with as just that, a revelation.

The discussion of this scene, as with many others in *8½*, must avoid analysis of particulars and questions of "realism," and rather explore synthesis and structure, and their effect upon the viewer. It is tempting, for instance, to accept Guido's words as the explanation of this last scene. Certainly it is relevant to the film, and to our understanding of him, when Guido says that seeking is more important than finding, and that one must accept life and people for what they are, not trying to idealize either. Moreover, the importance of Guido's words are to some extent supported by the use of the tower. As the child Guido draws back the drapes, all the people of his life walk down out of the tower. They descend from that ethereal, idealistic state where Guido once floated and come "down to earth," in order to dance around a circle of unity. One could comment on the "significance" of the white clothes of the people and the fact that Claudia is not seen in the final dance, although it should be noted that it is her face and her movement which immediately precede some of Guido's most perceptive statements about himself.

Such analytic approaches do indeed provide insights into the understanding of the last scene or even the entire film. But although it is misleading to talk about what something "represents" in a Fellini film, an analysis of the overall contour and impression of the last scene does seem important and worthwhile. From such a perspective the words that Guido speaks are just his attempts to verbalize about an experience he has just had or is having. The words are the result of an insight, not its cause. By the same token, the white clothes can be looked upon as a simple way of visualizing a definite change in the status of the people, at least in relation to Guido.

The last two scenes of the film can best be understood as an experience which begins in paranoid frenzy and ends with celebration, the simple flute-playing of a child. There are definite ellipses in this process, but it does occur. At the beginning of the two scenes Guido was trying to escape and by the end of the two scenes he has taken command, using a megaphone to direct the players and crew and then joining the people in the dance. That is the overall experience which the scenes impress upon the viewer.

The change in Guido is presented in the form of a spectacle, one in which director, actors, viewers, crew, and film equipment (lights, megaphone) are seen simultaneously. The experience has no tenses but the present; it is immediate. For Guido the confusion of life and spectacle has momentarily ended. Life has become spectacle. The appearance of the clowns and the circus ring support this impression. The film about a film has become the film. The last scene brings together, in one spectacle, what was previously incoherent, disparate, and confused, and does so in a purely filmic way—the only way possible for Guido.

As life becomes spectacle, it is interesting to note that the close-up emphasis on Guido becomes long-shot de-emphasis. The camera frees him, pulling back to more distant wider views which see him within a community of people. The scale is readjusted and he becomes part of a world. The off-screen space has been incorporated into the on-screen space. Claustrophobia gives way to panorama; the jail of self opens to a world of spatial horizons and human community.

On a very "realistic," factual level, the viewer does not know precisely what happened at the press conference (regarding the experience of the film; of course, what happens is what is shown) and what decision Guido might have made to lead to the dismantling of the tower. That earlier dismantling did not preclude the presence of motion picture lights and cameras on the tower for the final scene. The viewer does not know the relationship between the aborted film and the one Guido is directing at the end of the film. All of these explanations are deliberately left ambiguous to focus attention on the central structure, which is Guido's movement from paralysis, fear, and frustration, on the one hand, to involvement, action, and direction on the other hand. The film presents Guido trying to escape at the press conference and it then presents him taking control of a situation.

What the viewer knows through experience is that what has been at times disparate, separated in space and time, gratuitous and fragmented, is now somehow woven together. The filmic space is now filled with the separate elements and they are unified by their simultaneous existence within the frame and their context. A filmic space which was formerly subject to internal implosions and external manipulations has now been given wholeness. This union, this celebration, this affirmation is articulated not only through spatial unity but also by the similarity of dress, the dance around the ring, the presence of the child Guido, and by "La passerella di addio," a version of the *8½* theme which includes almost every musical motif in the film. The epiphany is then an affirmation and celebration, however simple, of unity, of spontaneity, of freedom, of innocence.

And how did this dramatic change occur? How did it happen that the film moved from a reluctant, estranged Guido to an active film director? On one level, of course, and the more rational one, there is some indication that something Guido did during or after the press conference helped to initiate the sequence of events. The link between such an action and the finale are tenuous, however. What is directly shown to the viewer is Maurice, the magician who earlier aided Maya. Waving his wand, he appears in front of the car and tells Guido that they are ready to begin. It is only after Maurice appears and speaks that Guido is led to a state of understanding and action. What really happens is that a transformation takes place, its beginning visualized through a magician, and that the transformation has very little to do with rational explanation. The transformation cannot be accounted for as the logical and necessary result of any actions and processes that have been developing in the film, at least not in the acceptable manner that dramatic action leads to a probable and neces- sary conclusion. One moment Guido has given up on his film and the next he is overcome with certain feelings that lead him to pick up the megaphone and direct the action. Nothing attempts to explain logically that change, except for Guido's verbal rationalizations of what he has experienced. The change in Guido (and no one should assume that it is permanent) comes as magically and mysteriously as any muse. He has not "earned" his salvation in any conventional sense. There has been a descent into Hell (the producer says, "We've been waiting for you three days") and now the dead person has arisen. The man who was once lifeless, fearful, and paranoid, threatened continually by unknown forces off-screen and trapped by a relentless camera, is now filled with energy, action, affirmation. It is an act of grace rather than of will.

All of Fellini's films have celebrated, in some form, such mystical and magical moments. In *La strada,* when Gelsomina's sense of life's meaning and purpose was most threatened, three clowns appeared out of nowhere in a field and she joined them as they played and marched. The references in *8½* to magic and mysticism help to pre- pare the viewer for such a transformation. This gift of grace is visualized primarily through the unity and movement in space of the major characters in the film, their joining in a circle to dance together, the camera's pulling back for lengthy shots of the entire scene, and also by Guido's willingness to pick up the megaphone, direct, and join in the dance.[27] Once salvation has been given to him, however tentative, he suddenly becomes capable of spontaneous and vigorous action. The boy inside the man has been freed and restored, not by design, deliberation, or development, but by an act of grace.

summary critique

Although *8½* won numerous awards, including seven silver ribbons in Italy, the Grand Prize at the 1963 Moscow Film Festival, and two American Academy Awards,[28] the critical response to the film was somewhat mixed.[29] Invariably, as with other Fellini films, the critical reaction fell into discernible categories. A number of critics felt that the work was too autobiographical and therefore not of sufficient universal interest. Some critics were—more perceptively—not so much concerned with the way that the film seemed to be about Fellini himself but with how deeply it explored certain recurrent themes in his work: the use of the circus at the end, the dance around the ring, the appearance of the clowns, the concern with what is appearance and what is reality, the absolute need for people to love and be loved, their need to be accepted and to accept themselves for what they are, the playful criticism of the church, the belief in miracles and grace, the celebration of the personal and idiosyncratic.[30]

Other commentators found the film deliberately confusing and inarticulate; they considered the mixture of kinds of experience not as deliberate and meaningful but as the product of a confused mind which had fumbled the attempt to elucidate itself. A number of other critics saw the film as having no meaning, by which they meant that the film did not lend itself to useful interpretation. They saw in it no socially important comment or unique ideas.

Some critics—actually very few—were amazed and delighted by the visual imagination revealed by the film and by the attempt to deal directly through the cinematic medium with the processes of the mind. They pointed out how the formal implosions of *8½* were not merely the workings of a confused director but an attempt to use cinematic strategies to relate directly the experience of the protagonist.

Exerpts from reviews reflecting all these various critical positions are given in the bibliography. Today, however, there is less concern over many aspects of *8½* that bothered critics when it was first released. The furor over the autobiographical aspects of the film has died down, and audiences are more willing to accept the pure visual pleasure it offers. There seems little reason now to dwell on the developing critical view. My own appreciation of Fellini's purpose and strategies is obvious in my consideration of the film in this volume, particularly at the beginning of the analysis section, and the interested reader will see how and where I differ from the critics quoted in the bibliography.

The most important criticism of *8½* is that it is shown, studied, and appreciated now, more than a decade after it was introduced. In the year before I began this study there were at least six separate commercial screenings in New York City alone. It is, of course, often shown by film societies and in cinema study courses. Enlightened in no small part by *8½* itself (and by its director's later work), viewers today are likely to accept its depiction of time and space as a filmic reality, rather than as a distortion of what they believe they experience or what they expect in a film.

Nowhere is this more evident than in a willingness to consider that the film may have, as do dreams and other forms, two endings: one that culminates in the seeming suicide and one that sees the young boy exit the circus ring. The possibility of a double ending, one a denial of life and one an affirmation, is quite acceptable and helps to illuminate the work. There is certainly no reason why only the last scene must be a film's ending. By having the affirmative action (the circus dance) follow the suicide, the filmmaker gives us some idea of his own preference without denying the darker side of his mind. By avoiding a neat and well-rounded ending, the filmmaker asks the viewer to share with him the ambiguity of life, the dialectic of contrary states. Moreover, a double ending confounds simple interpretation, as has been the case throughout *8½,* and throws the viewer back upon his own direct experience of the film.

Indeed, such are the main virtues of *8½* and all those films which ask us to confront them as films, rather that as mirrors of the world or of what is expected in a film. From such films we learn anew to see, to reexamine our prejudices and preconceptions—about what a film is and what life is.

a Fellini filmography
discography
bibliography
rental source
notes

a Fellini filmography

A complete filmography would include all of the films on which Fellini worked—as writer, actor, as director. Such a list would be long, since Fellini was active from 1939 on. The present filmography includes only those films or episodes which Fellini himself directed. The reader who wishes to know about Fellini's other film activities should consult the *Filmlexicon degli autori e delle opere,* volume 2 (Rome: Edizioni di Bianco e Nero, 1959), 650, the *Enciclopedia dello spettacolo,* volume 5 (Rome: Casa Editrice le Maschere, 1958), 143–46, or the filmographies in books on Fellini by Suzanne Budgen, Gilbert Salachas, and others noted in the bibliography.

1950 *Variety Lights (Luci del varietà).* Produced by Fellini and Alberto Lattuada for Capitolium Films.

1952 *The White Sheik (Lo sceicco bianco).* Produced by Luigi Rovere.

1953 *I vitelloni (The Loafers;* or *The Young and the Passionate).* Produced by Lorenzo Pegoraro for Peg Films–Cité Films.

The Matrimonial Agency (Un'agenzia matrimoniale), an episode in *Love in the City (Amore in città).* Produced by Cesare Zavattini for Faro Film.

1954 *La strada (The Road).* Produced by Carlo Ponti and Dino De Laurentiis.

1955 *Il bidone (The Swindle).* Produced by Titanus for Mario De Vecchi Films.

1956 *The Nights of Cabiria (Le notti di Cabiria).* Produced by Dino De Laurentiis.

1959 *La dolce vita.* Produced by Giuseppe Amato and Angelo Rizzoli for Riama Film–Pathé Consortium Cinéma.

1961 *The Temptations of Doctor Antonio (Le tentazioni del dottor Antonio),* an episode in *Boccaccio '70.* Produced by Carlo Ponti.

1963 *8½ (Otto e mezzo).* Produced by Angelo Rizzoli.

1965 *Juliet of the Spirits (Giulietta degli spiriti).* Produced by Angelo Rizzoli for Federiz.

1967 *Toby Dammit,* an episode in *Spirits of the Dead (Tre passi nel delirio).* Produced by Les Films Marceau–Cocinor.

1969 *Fellini's Satyricon.* Produced by Alberto Grimaldi.

Fellini: A Director's Notebook. Produced for NBC-TV by Peter Goldfarb.

1970 *The Clowns.* Produced by Elio Scardamaglia and Ugo Guerra.
–71

1972 *Fellini's Roma.* Produced by Ultra Film.

1973 *Amarcord (I Remember).* Produced by Franco Cristaldi.

FILM ABOUT FELLINI

1970 *Ciao, Federico!* Directed by Gideon Bachmann. Produced by Victor Herbert.

discography

Joseph E. Levine presents Federico Fellini's *8½,* Music by Nino Rota, Original Film Soundtrack, copyright 1963 RCA International, FSO-6.

Side One
La passerella di "Otto e Mezzo" (Nino Rota)
Cimitero (Nino Rota)/Gigolette (F. Lehár)/Cadillac (Nino Rota)/
     Carlotta's Galop (Nino Rota)
E poi (Walzer) (Nino Rota)
L'illusionista (Nino Rota)
Concertino alle terme (Rossini-Tchaikovsky)
Nell'ufficio produzione di "Otto e Mezzo" (Nino Rota)
Ricordo d'infanzia (Nino Rota)/Discesa al fanghi (Nino Rota)

Side Two
Guido e Luisa—Nostalgic Swing (Nino Rota)
Carlotta's Galop (Nino Rota)
L'Harem (Nino Rota)
Rivolta nell'Harem (Wagner)/La ballerina pensionata (Ça c'est
     Paris) (Padilla)/La conferenza stampa del regista (Nino Rota)
La passerella di addio (Nino Rota)

bibliography

This is a working bibliography; that is, the items are selected and annotated with the hope that they will be read along with the text, in order to understand more about Fellini and *8½*. Since there is so much written material on Fellini, I have limited the entries below, with few exceptions, to items that pertain directly to *8½*. Those who wish to pursue the subject further should consult the various bibliographies in the books noted below and also the following: Richard Dyer MacCann and Edward Perry, *The New Film Index* (E. P. Dutton, 1975); *FIAF Index to Film Periodicals* (R. R. Bowker, 1972–   ); George Rehrauer, *Cinema Booklist* (Scarecrow Press, 1972); and Mel Schuster, *Motion Picture Directors* (Scarecrow Press, 1973), 140–42.

1. BOOKS AND ARTICLES

Agel, Geneviève. *Les chemins de Fellini.* Paris: Éditions du Cerf, 1956. An interpretation of Fellini's work which stresses Christian themes and symbols.

Bachmann, Gideon. "Federico Fellini." *Cinemages.* (1973). Entire issue devoted to Fellini and to *Ciao, Federico!* the film Bachmann made during the shooting of *Satyricon.* Includes credits, complete script, story of the film's production, an interview with Bachmann, sampling of press comments, and a lecture on Fellini given by Bachmann at Harvard.

Bachmann, Gideon. "Fellini 8½." *Film Journal* [Melbourne], no. 21 (April 1963), 116–18. Observations about *8½* and Fellini made by a critic and friend. "The intermanipulation of time achieves the surreal effect of a lived dream and a dreamt reality all at once, with three intermingled 'actions' progressing at the same time: the world of the film director who is the hero of the film, his dream world, and the world within the film which he is shooting. Fellini separates the levels of these worlds only through costuming—identical costumes are worn by identical actors, but they are either white or black depending on the degrees of 'reality' they indicate in the particular emotional situation depicted."

Baker, Peter. "Eight and a Half." *Films and Filming,* 10, no. 1 (October 1963), 21. "The most satisfying thing about *8½* is his skill in getting under the skin of the central character. . . . Everything about *8½* is technically proficient. . . . What is so despicable about it is the final abdication. . . . He ends by questioning if audiences want truth, indeed, whether they want life."

Bazin, André. "Cabiria: The Voyage to the End of Neorealism." *What is Cinema?* Essays selected and translated by Hugh Gray (Berkeley: University of California Press, 1971), 2:83–92. An early critical analysis of Fellini's work which provides a clear insight into the role of grace and the fortuitous nature of the narrative. This English translation of Bazin's work does not include three other essays on Fellini, dealing with *La strada, Il bidone,* and *I vitelloni,* which appear in volume 4 of the original French collection of Bazin's essays, *Qu'est-ce que le cinéma?* (Paris: Éditions du Cerf, 1962), 122–33, 143–45.

Benderson, Albert Edward. *Critical Approaches to Federico Fellini's 8½.* (New York: Arno Press, 1974.) A detailed analysis of the film, stressing the contextual and archetypal approaches. Bibliography.

Bennett, Joseph. "Italian Film: Failure and Emergence." *Kenyon Review,* 26, no. 4 (Autumn 1964), 738–47. "I think that *8½* is the worst film ever made by a major Italian film director. It is a disgusting piece of self-exhibitionism; it wallows in self-indulgence and self-abuse. Its pretentiousness is totally gagging."

Boyer, Deena. *The Two Hundred Days of 8½.* Translated by Charles Markmann (New York: Macmillan, 1964). A day-to-day account of the production. An afterword by Dwight MacDonald stresses the positive aspects of the film. "It is more Handel than Beethoven—objective and classical in spirit as against the romantic subjectivism we are accustomed to. It's all there, right on the surface, like a Veronese or a Tiepolo." The afterword is especially useful not only as strong statement in favor of *8½* but also for the way in which it critiques other statements made about the film. Reprinted in *Dwight MacDonald on the Movies* (Englewood Cliffs, N.J.: Prentice Hall, 1969), 15–31.

Boyum, Joy Gould, and Adrienne Scott (eds.). *Film as Film: Critical Responses to Film Art* (Boston: Allyn and Bacon, 1971), 172–80. Reprints of three reviews published at the time of the American release. John Simon, writing in the *New Leader,* finds *8½* "a disheartening fiasco." It is poor autobiography, sheds no light on the problem it poses, and lacks solid intellectual content. Robert Hatch, in *The Nation,* says "Fellini's ability to make a film flow with the sparkle, surprise and occasional peril of a quick stream is the key to his distinction. . . . The finale, for which everyone in the huge cast joins hands in a giant ring-around-a-rosie, to the music of a clown band, is visually most engaging, but I doubt that it epitomizes Fellini's philosophy, or stands for anything more than a good camera shot." In *Saturday Review,* Hollis Alpert notes that "Fellini has taken a personal and most difficult subject, treated it with all the imagination he is capable of, and fashioned a film of the highest distinction."

Budgen, Suzanne. *Fellini* (London: British Film Institute Education Department, 1966). A monograph on Fellini's work through *Juliet of the Spirits.* Extracts from two interviews and the script of *La strada.* Thorough filmography includes cast and other credits. The analysis of *8½,* although highly thematic and focused too much on the last scene, is careful and considerate.

Carey, Gary. *"8½:* Director in Mid-Journey." *The Seventh Art,* 1, no. 4 (Fall 1963), 12, 27, 28.

Casty, Alan. *Development of the Film: An Interpretive History* (New York: Harcourt Brace Jovanovich, 1973), 291–301. "The full protean flow of his splintered experience of his own life is given psychological unity by the film's mixing of tones and moods— satiric and romantic, comic and desperate—and by its witty interplay of Guido's varied realities. . . . But the affirmation of the ending is still part of the ironic counterpoint of the film's total texture, its truth as fantasy still not acted out in the external interpersonal area of reality."

Cohen, Roberta. "A Fresh Interpretation of Fellini's 8½." *Film* [London], no. 38 (Winter 1963), 18–19. "He . . . shoots himself! . . . In the last scene of the movie, one of a heavenly reconciliation, Guido understands himself at last."

Cook, Alton. Review. *New York World-Telegram and Sun,* June 26, 1963, 26.

Cowie, Peter (ed.). "Federico Fellini." *International Film Guide: 1965* (London: Tantivy Press, 1965), 11–14. Brief survey of his work; filmography.

Crist, Judith. *The Private Eye, the Cowboy and the Very Naked Girl* (Chicago: Holt, Rinehart & Winston, 1968), 14–16. Reprint of her original review. *8½* "is a masterwork of one of the great directors. . . . Dazzled by the technique and the mind in control of it, we watch and listen with fascination, captives for the duration. And at the end we are instantly freed by the sudden realization that the heart has not been touched or the spirit moved."

Crowther, Bosley. "Review of *8½*." *New York Times,* June 26, 1963, 36. "Mr. Fellini has managed to compress so much drollery and wit, so much satire on social aberrations, so much sardonic comment on sex and, indeed, when you come right down to it, even a bit of travesty of Freud, that it pains me to note that he hasn't thought his film through to a valid end."

Dillard, R. H. W. "If We Were All Devils: Fellini's *Satyricon* as Horror Film." *Contempora,* 1, no. 5 (1971), 26–33. Contains useful bibliography on Fellini, compiled by George P. Garrett.

"Director on the Couch." *Time,* June 28, 1963, 82. While *8½* is a "fascinating ride down Fellini's stream of consciousness," he need not have shown publicly his "liberating experience."

"Dizzy Doings on a Set: Making of a Movie—*8½*." *Life,* July 19, 1963. 95–97. Primarily illustrations.

Dyer, Peter John. "Review of *8½*." *Monthly Film Bulletin,* 30, no. 357 (October 1963), 140. "The whole may add up to a magnificent folly, but it is too singular, too candid, too vividly and insistently alive to be judged as being in any way diminishing."

Eason, Patrick. "Notes on Double Structure and the Films of Fellini." *Cinema* [Cambridge], no. 2 (March 1969), 22–24. *La strada, Il bidone,* and *8½* are discussed. "Fellini has developed a double structure in which the film is organized either on two different levels or in two different parts, the aesthetic response to the film being directly attributable to the interaction of these two levels or parts. *8½* is the most successful example of this structure: here the tension between Guido's inner life and his work is externalised in the film he is making and the women in his life— form and content are indivisible."

Estève, Michel. "Federico Fellini: *8½*." *Études cinématographiques,* nos. 28–29 (Winter 1963). Entire issue devoted to *8½* with seven articles by serious critics. Here and elsewhere (Metz, John Russell Taylor), attention is given to comparing *8½* with some of the work of André Gide. Also includes a sampling of other critical response, filmography, and a bibliography which is especially useful for its inclusion of French and Italian reviews and articles on *8½*. Illustrated.

Favazza, A. "Fellini: Analyst Without Portfolio." *Man and the Movies.* Edited by W. R. Robinson (Baton Rouge: Louisiana State University, 1967), 180–90. A psychiatrist deals with Fellini's work, especially *8½* and *Juliet,* explaining that creativity (libido) and religion are the director's basic themes. "Consider *8½*. Is this anything other than the story of a man (Fellini) suffering from a pathological depression and his attempts to dispel the oppressive effect? Creativity was stifled. . . . We see the various mechanisms Fellini used to alleviate his depression: Desensitization through recall, verbalization, and assimilation of past painful experiences; desensitization through association of experiences which have aroused anxiety with new pleasurable experiences; and, most powerfully, de-repression of past painful experiences."

Gessner, Robert. *The Moving Image* (New York: E. P. Dutton & Co., 1968), 259–61, et passim. "Two main streams surge through the film [*8½*]: the narrative line concerning the frustrations over the pending film production and a parallel line composed of flashback dreams and psychic fantasies, meant to explore childhood motivations or adult escapes."

Gilbert, Justin. Review. *New York Mirror,* June 26, 1963, A2.

Gill, Brendan. "Current Cinema." *New Yorker,* June 29, 1963, 62. "It is marvelous. . . . *8½* is a comedy, and the hero's plight and eventual salvation are, to an uncanny degree, disguised manifestations of joy."

Gilliatt, Penelope. "Fantastic Fellini." *London Observer,* August 25, 1963, 17. "*8½* . . . has been made by a man whose genius for film making spills out of his ears, and I hope its courage isn't going to be dismissed because it is flamboyant and comic."

Hale, Wanda. Review. *New York Daily News,* June 26, 1963, 62.

Harcourt, Peter. "The Secret Life of Federico Fellini." *Six European Directors* (Baltimore: Penguin Books, 1974), 183–211. Expanded and revised version of an essay by the same title published in *Film Quarterly,* 19, no. 3 (Spring 1966), 4–19. An important, perceptive analysis of all of Fellini's films before *Amarcord,* stressing their thematic consistency, the subliminal nature of the imagery and its impact, the particular worldview, and other topics. *8½* is analyzed in detail because it is regarded as a key film in his work and because it "is one of the greatest films of all time." Speaking of the final dance around the circus ring, the author comments "we have the mystic circle of eternity, ancient symbol of the Christian church incorporated by Dante. And so too we have the final consummate image of movement without direction, dancing round and round for ever in an infinity of shared acceptance."

Hirschman, Jack. "8½." *Film Quarterly,* 17, no. 1 (Fall 1963), 43–46. "Fellini has successfully arrived at the heart of what the film (as poem, painting, book, play) was destined for: the question of illusion and/or reality. . . . Fellini *does* get his film on film, but in such a compositional way that we are made to feel it shot through with that taproot intuition, which is the process of creation itself."

Holland, Norman. "Fellini's *8½;* Holland's *11.*" *Hudson Review,* 16, no. 3 (Autumn 1963), 429–36. A careful analysis of the film. "Autobiography can be fun, and the most exquisite moments in *8½* are the most intensely autobiographical. . . . The trouble seems to come from another quarter—moral and intellectual content."

Hughes, Eileen Lanouette. *On the Set of Fellini Satyricon* (New York: William Morrow & Co., 1971). A day-to-day account of the filming.

Huss, Roy, and Norman Silverstein. *The Film Experience: Elements of Motion Picture Art* (New York: Dell, 1968), 46–47, 94–98. "As Guido moves from left to right with the camera tracking him, he meets all the people of his past life moving in procession from right to left. . . . When Guido joins the dancers, a harmonious feeling is rhythmically enhanced by the subjugation of Guido's individual lateral movement to the massive and overwhelming circular one: thematically, the sequence shows that Guido has come to terms with those forces of his past who are dancing about him and with whom he conjoins."

Kael, Pauline. "*8½:* Confessions of a Movie Director." *I Lost It at the Movies* (New York: Little, Brown & Co., 1965), 261–66. "Someone's fantasy life is perfectly good material for a movie *if* it is imaginative and fascinating in itself, or if it illuminates his non-fantasy life in some interesting way. But *8½* is neither; it's surprisingly like the confectionary dreams of Hollywood heroines, transported by a hack's notions of Freudian anxiety and wish fulfillment."

Kauffmann, Stanley. *A World on Film: Criticism and Comment* (New York: A Delta Book, 1967), 322–25. Reprint of his July 13, 1963, review in the *New Republic*. "In . . . execution I cannot remember a more brilliant film. In image, visual ingenuity, subtlety of pace, sardonic humour, it is stunning. . . . But when we ask what the theme of the film really is, what the director learns from his crisis about his crisis, what the resolution really means, the answers are less satisfactory. . . . Virtuosity has an aesthetic value of its own, whether it is coloratura singing or fantastic pirouettes or *trompe-l'oeil* painting, and when it is as overwhelming as Fellini's virtuosity, one can be moved by it very nearly as much as by art that 'says' something."

Kinder, Marsha, and Beverle Houston. *Close-Up* (New York: Harcourt Brace Jovanovich, 1972), 246–54. "*8½*'s focus on the creative process, its subtle mix of past and present, reality, memory and fantasy, and its allusions to his other films—all contribute to Fellini's success in using the medium to express a subjective and autobiographical vision."

Kovács, Steven. "Fellini's 'Toby Dammit': A Study of Characteristic Themes and Techniques." *Journal of Aesthetics and Art Criticism*, 31, no. 2 (Winter 1972), 255–61. One of the things which is characteristic of Fellini's work is that "he first analyzes and then synthesizes the filmmaking process."

Lane, John Francis. "A Case of Artistic Inflation." *Sight and Sound*, 32, no. 3 (Summer 1963), 130–35. On the Italian cinema in general, stressing the pretentiousness of the subject matter. *8½* is cited as a case in point. "Having set themselves to tackle themes which have awed great men of letters, they proceed to embark on a sort of D'Annunzian artistic holiday."

Lane, John Francis. "The Shake Up." *Films and Filming,* 9, no. 8 (May 1963), 55. "Fellini's 'bomb.' "

Lerman, Leo. Review. *Mademoiselle,* September 1963, 62.

Lewis, Leon. "Fellini: The Psychology of the Self." *The Landscape of Contemporary Cinema*. Edited by William Sherman and Leon Lewis (Buffalo: Spectrum Press, 1967), 9–12. "Fellini's *8½* is a masterpiece. . . . The only real problem is the conclusion. The frivolous ending is in no way even a suggestion of a resolution of the problems Fellini poses."

Linden, George W. *Reflections on the Screen* (Belmont, California: Wadsworth Publishing Co., 1970), 10, 231, 258–63, et passim. Contains several perceptive references to *8½* and other Fellini films. The "strength of weakness" is seen as a theme in *La strada* and *8½,* for instance. "Here is a man [Guido/Fellini] who laughs at himself *seriously* and is unafraid to be permeable. In this sense, *8½* is an essay on the strength of weakness. Thus, the film can and does reach to the I and reveals it through tonal dialogue, unreflective gesture, and the force of presence. Unlike pottery, the self, when broken and repaired, often gains in strength." Elsewhere the author explores five separate levels of reality in the film and asserts that the theme is the "difficulty if not impossibility, of emotional commitment in the modern world."

Maddocks, Melvin. Review. *Christian Science Monitor,* June 26, 1963.

Mekas, Jonas. Review comments. *Village Voice,* June 27, 1963.

Metz, Christian. "Mirror Construction in Fellini's *8½.*" *Film Language: A Semiotics of the Cinema.* Translated by Michael Taylor (New York: Oxford University Press, 1974), 228–34. Drawing upon the articles published in *Études cinématographiques,* nos. 28–29, Metz builds an important case for *8½.* It "is a film that is *doubly doubled*—and when one speaks of it as having a mirror construction, it is really a double mirror construction one should be talking about. It is not only a film about the cinema, it is a film about a film that is presumably itself about the cinema; it is not only a film about a director, but a film about a director who is reflecting himself onto his film. . . . *8½* is the film of *8½* being made; *the 'film in the film' is, in this case, the film itself.*" The most convincing literary antecedent "is André Gide's *Paludes,* since it is about a novelist writing *Paludes.*"

Moravia, Alberto. "Federico Fellini: Director as Protagonist." *Atlas,* 5, no. 4 (April 1963), 246–48. Celebrates the vitality and originality with which Fellini tells "us how and why he has nothing further to say. . . . *8½* indicates a crisis and the successful resolution of it."

Myhers, John. "Fellini's Continuing Autobiography." *Cinema* [Beverly Hills] 6, no. 2 (1970), 40–41. An attempt to relate episodes in Fellini's life to episodes in *Satyricon*.

Ortmayer, Roger. "Fellini's Film Journey." *Three European Directors*. Edited by James M. Wall (Grand Rapids, Mich.: Eerdmans Publishing Co., 1973), 65–107.

Paolucci, Anne. "The Italian Film: Antonioni, Fellini, Bolognini." *Massachusetts Review,* 7, no. 3 (Summer 1966), 556–67. "In *8½* we see the drama of life with all its confusion of values, its sordid pleasures, its human mistakes, the short-lived joys which haunt the memory but can never be recaptured."

Pechter, William S. "*8½* Times Two." *Twenty-four Times a Second* (New York: Harper & Row, 1971), 77–84. A careful analysis which accounts for much in the film, particularly the nature of its comic element and the way in which the film is like an interior monologue. "Yet, rather than confusing or stalemating our response, this blurring of boundaries [between kinds of reality] has the effect of heightening our awareness of both the rational content of dream and fantasy and the fantastic element in what we call reality."

Perry, Ted. "Signifiers in Fellini's *8½*." *Forum Italicum,* 6, no. 1 (March 1972), 79–86.

Price, James. "*8½*: A Quest for Ecstasy." *London Magazine,* n.s. 3, no. 8 (November 1963), 58–62. Objects to the repetition of certain clichés—the clowns, the dance at the end—but praises certain aspects, such as the satire and the imagery.

Renzi, Renzo. *Federico Fellini* (Parma: Guanda, 1956). Brief biographical and critical analysis up through *Nights of Cabiria*.

Review. *Catholic World,* September 1963, 395–96.

Review. *Commonweal,* July 12, 1963, 425.

Review. *Newsweek,* June 24, 1963, 112–14.

Rhode, Eric. "Federico Fellini." *Tower of Babel: Speculations on the Cinema* (London: Weidenfeld and Nicolson, 1966), 121–34. "Guido must try to free himself, especially from mere doctrine. His art, he realizes, must include all his past obsessions, all that makes up his present self. The irrational must enter so that the web of false symbolism, of false meanings, may be destroyed, and the true candid images emerge." An important essay which, by posing several polarities at work in Fellini's

films—the provinces versus Rome, the Rome which gave birth
to European civilization versus the Christian Rome that replaced
the ancient one—almost predicts the films that followed: *Satyri-*
con, Roma. The author takes to task the critics of Fellini who,
consciously or not, see him as failing to live up to the standards
of Neorealism. No one lived up to those standards because they
were inherently naive. "Because of this, Fellini's search for the
authentic self through fantasy takes on a historical significance."
But the emphasis upon fantasy is articulated through a strong
sense of locality. "Fellini has a feeling for the genius of a place
—for those gods and demons who inhabit a specific locality."

Rhode, Eric. "Film Reviews: *8½.*" *Sight and Sound,* 32, no. 4
(Autumn 1963), 193. For the most part a review which praises
the film for its inventiveness. "Guido may confront his inner
world but he fails to confront his social obligations. . . . None-
theless, though he can't face up to the total case, we must be
grateful to Fellini for having presented so much of it, and with
such flair and exuberance."

Richardson, Robert. "Wastelands: The Breakdown of Order." *Liter-*
ature and Film (Bloomington: Indiana University Press, 1969),
106–16. The idea of the loss of order pervades modern poetry
and film. Fellini and T.S. Eliot are symptomatic of this theme
and their work is compared. "The work of Fellini and Eliot is
similar in ways that range from the fortuitous to the important,
but beyond particular likenesses of theme, image, tone, or technique, there is, I think, an overiding similarity [which] I would
describe as an aesthetic of disparity." The formal equivalent of
disparity is montage, present in both artists.

Rondi, Brunello. *Il cinema di Fellini* (Rome: Edizioni de Bianco e
Nero, 1965). Fellini's friend and frequent collaborator provides
an insider's perceptive analysis of each film through *Juliet of the*
Spirits. Filmography.

Rondi, Gian Luigi. *Italian Cinema Today* (New York: Hill and
Wang, 1966), 92–111. Brief, laudatory essay with numerous
illustrations.

Salachas, Gilbert. *Federico Fellini.* Translated by Rosalie Siegel
(New York: Crown Publishers, 1969). Broad spectrum of material on Fellini. Biographical and critical essay by Salachas,
large sampling of comments made by Fellini in interviews,

excerpts from screenplays and film treatments, variety of statements made by critics, friends, and co-workers. Useful filmography and bibliography.

Schickel, Richard. *Movies: The History of an Art and an Institution* (New York: Basic Books, 1964), 153–55. "Embraced by the critics, it [*8½*] represents, in fact, the death of the cinema as a public art, whose function has been to hold a mirror up to the physical world not the inner world of the creator."

Solmi, Angelo. *Fellini.* Translated by Elizabeth Greenwood (New York: Humanities Press, 1968). A very personal account of Fellini and his work. Includes a review of the key themes, a biographical section which treats not only Fellini's life before filmmaking but also recounts the making of each film to *8½*. Interpretation, knowledge of each production experience, and personal feelings are offered together. Bibliography and filmography.

Taylor, John Russell. *Cinema Eye, Cinema Ear: Some Key Filmmakers of the Sixties* (New York: Hill and Wang, 1964), 15–51, 230–33, 279. A cogent biographical and critical statement on Fellini, stressing the thematic aspects of his films and their relationships to one another. *8½,* as the last film discussed, "is a series of attempts by a disorientated intellectual to find his way, to find a truth, about himself and the world around him, by which he can live. Back-to-the-womb, a contracting-out of the complexities and discomforts of adult life, is only one way of dealing with his problems, and evidently right from the start one which is not practicable: even in his childhood the seeds of shame are sown. . . . In *8½* Fellini clearly shows himself to be what we have always at least half suspected him of being, a baroque fantasist whose private world has nothing more than a few accidents of time and place in common with any 'real' world." Filmography.

Williams, F. "Fellini's Voices." *Film Quarterly,* 21, no. 3 (Spring 1968) 21–25. Although devoted almost entirely to *Juliet of the Spirits,* this is one of the few attempts to discuss the nature and function of dialogue in Fellini's films.

Winsten, Archer. Review. *New York Post,* June 26, 1963.

Winston, Douglas Garrett. *The Screenplay as Literature* (Rutherford, N.J.: Fairleigh Dickinson Press, 1973), 140–61. An analysis of

Fellini's work which stresses the psychoanalytic techniques evident in his films, particularly *8½*.

Wood, Robin. "The Question of Fellini Continues." *December,* 9, nos. 2–3 (1967), 140. About *La dolce vita* and *8½*. "For all the dazzling and unflagging invention and virtuosity and . . . the disarming humor, the grandeur of spirit is almost entirely lacking."

2. INTERVIEWS AND ARTICLES IN WHICH FELLINI DISCUSSES HIMSELF AND HIS WORK.

Bachmann, Gideon. "Federico Fellini: An Interview." *Film: Book One.* Edited by Robert Hughes (New York: Grove Press, 1959), 97–105.

Bachmann, Gideon. "How I Make Films: An Interview with Federico Fellini." *U.S. Camera World Annual,* 1967, 139–41, 202–05.

Bachmann, Gideon. "Interview with Federico Fellini." *Sight and Sound,* 33, no. 2 (Spring 1964), 82–87.

Fellini, Federico. "*8½* Interview." *Cinema* [BeverlyHills], 1, no. 5 (1963), 19–22.

Fellini, Federico. "I Was Born for the Cinema." *Film Comment,* 4 no. 1 (Fall 1966), 77–84. Interview conducted by Irving R. Levine.

Fellini, Federico. "My Dolce Vita." *Oui* (March 1973), 35–36, 108–10.   "I had a magical childhood, dominated by the Sea, the Circus, and the Church."

Fellini, Federico. "9½: A Self Portrait of the Movie Director as an Artist." *Show* (May 1964), 86, 105. "It seems to me that this must be my *mythos:* to try and throw off my back the upbringing I have had; that is, to try to uneducate myself in order to recapture a virginal availability and a new type of personal, individual education."

"Interview: Federico Fellini." *Playboy* (February 1966), 55–66. "In *8½,* society's norms and rules imprisoned Guido in his boyhood with a sense of guilt and frustration. . . . The return of Guido to life in *8½* is not a defeat. . . . He is at peace with himself at last—free to accept himself as he is, not as he wished he were or might have been. That is the optimistic finale to *8½*."

Kast, Pierre. "Giulietta and Federico: Visits with Fellini." *Cahiers du*

Cinema in English, no. 5 (1966), 24–33. An interview with Fellini, mainly about *Juliet of the Spirits.* Some personal observations by the interviewer, general remarks about other films, including *8½,* and the repetition of Fellini's statement about the intention which he sees throughout his films: "it is the attempt to create an emancipation from conventional schemes, a liberation from moral rules; that is to say the attempt to retrieve an authenticity of life rhythm, of life modes, of vital cadences, which is opposed to an inauthentic form of life." Originally appeared in *Cahiers du cinéma* (March 1965) and reprinted in Andrew Sarris, *Interviews with Film Directors* (New York: Bobbs-Merrill, 1967), 141–54.

Ross, Lillian. "Profiles: 10½." *New Yorker,* October 30, 1965. Profile of Fellini in the form of a movie script.

Samuels, Charles Thomas. "Federico Fellini." *Encountering Directors* (New York: G. P. Putnam's Sons, 1972), 117–41. Excerpted in *Atlantic,* April 1972.

Silke, James (ed.). "Federico Fellini." *Discussion* (American Film Institute), no. 1 (1970). Interview, mainly about *Satyricon,* with filmography and bibliography.

Walter, Eugene. "Dinner with Fellini." *Transatlantic Review,* no. 17 (Autumn 1964), 47–50. "When he began shooting *8½,* he took a little piece of brown paper tape and stuck it near the viewfinder of the camera. Written on it was: *Remember That This is a Comic Film.*"

Walter, Eugene. "Federico Fellini: Wizard of Film." *Atlantic,* December 1965, 62–67.

3. SCREENPLAYS.

Fellini, Federico. *Early Screenplays.* Translated by Judith Green (New York: Orion Press, 1971). English translation of the screenplays for *Variety Lights* and *The White Sheik.*

Fellini, Federico. *8½.* Edited by Camilla Cederna (Bologna: Cappelli editore, 1965). The Italian screenplay and an introductory essay by Cederna, commenting on the production of the film. Appendix contains the screenplay of *Le tentazioni del dottor Antonio.* Illustrated.

Fellini, Federico. *Fellini's Satyricon.* Edited by Dario Zanelli. Translated by Eugene Walter and John Matthews (New York: Bal-

lantine Books, 1970). Screenplay and credits. Includes three
additional articles which help to clarify Fellini's intentions. Of
special interest is "Documentary of a Dream," a dialogue between Fellini and Alberto Moravia.

Fellini, Federico. *Juliet of the Spirits.* Edited by Tullio Kezich.
Translated by Howard Greenfield (New York: Orion Press,
1965). Introduction by Kezich, "The Long Interview" with
Fellini by Kezich, the original screenplay, and a transcription of
the final film.

Fellini, Federico. *La Dolce Vita.* Translated by Oscar DeLiso and
Bernard Shir-Cliff (New York: Ballantine Books, 1961).
English translation of the screenplay, including a reprint of a
review by Hollis Alpert. Illustrated.

"Special Fellini." *L'Avant-Scène du Cinéma,* no. 63 (1966). *8½*
screenplay in French, including some scenes which were shot
but later cut out. Brief survey of the critical response to *8½,*
Fellini filmography, quotes from several interviews with Fellini,
and some information on *Juliet of the Spirits.* Illustrated.

Fellini, Federico. *Three Screenplays.* Translated by Judith Green
(New York: Orion Press, 1970). English translations of screen-
plays for *I vitelloni, Il bidone, The Temptations of Doctor
Antonio.*

rental source

A 16mm print, with English subtitles, is available from CCM Films,
34 MacQuesten Parkway South, Mount Vernon, New York 10550.
Telephone (914) 664-5051.

notes

1. Various commentaries on the film suggest that the root word is
   anima, and that the formula (according to a scheme Fellini
   worked out with childhood friends to devise their own language)

is to follow each vowel of *anima* with an *s* and then repeat the vowel in order to achieve "Asa Nisi Masa." Deena Boyer, in *The Two Hundred Days of 8½* (New York: Macmillan, 1964), 70, reports that *Anima* was once considered as the title of the film. The use of the word is very tantalizing and tempts the critic to explore extensively the psychoanalytic aspects of *8½*, especially in Jungian thought. See Jung's discussion of the term in his collected papers or in *Psyche and Symbol* (New York: Doubleday, 1958). In this same context, the reader who is interested in exploring further the psychoanalytic aspects of the film should consult Sigmund Freud, "Symbolism in Dreams," *A General Introduction to Psychoanalysis* (New York: Garden City Publishing Co., 1938), 135–50, and Sigmund Freud, The Relation of the Poet to Day-Dreaming," *On Creativity and the Unconscious: Papers on the Psychology of Art, Literature, Love and Religion* (New York: Harper & Row, 1958), 44–54. See also the citations and annotations for Benderson, Favazza, Kael, Taylor, and Winston in the bibliography.

2. The name supposedly given during Fellini's childhood to a local prostitute who sold herself to the fishermen in return for what was left in their sardine nets. In that area (Rimini, Romagna), sardines are called *saraghine*.

3. A thorough understanding of Fellini's work requires that this point be emphasized and appreciated. In almost all of his films, Fellini's name appears in the credits for story and screenplay, along with those of his frequent collaborators.

4. See the citation and annotation for Linden in the bibliography.

5. See the citation and annotation for Harcourt in the bibliography.

6. See note 30.

7. In autumn 1960 Fellini wrote a letter to Brunello Rondi in which he outlined the proposed film. See, for instance, Angelo Solmi, *Fellini* (New York: Humanities Press, 1968), 164. It is this letter which is used to refute suspicions that *8½*, in form or locale, was influenced by Resnais' *Last Year at Marienbad*. The letter is reproduced by Camilla Cederna in the volume she edited, Federico Fellini, *8½* (Bologna: Cappelli editore, 1965), 20–27.

8. Ingmar Bergman's noted 1957 production, *Wild Strawberries*, also sometimes confounds temporal modes, as when Borg walks

into his own childhood memories. There are other interesting similarities with *8½*. Both films open with a dream and end in a dance, for instance. Fellini's admiration for Bergman has often been noted.

9. Quoted in the annotation for Metz in the bibliography.

10. Since there are so many scenes in *8½*, I have listed them individually and numbered them, even though the lines of distinction are not always clear. The scene titles and the decision as to when one scene ends and another begins are primarily my own and are based on repeated viewings of American release prints, kindly made available for my study by CCM Films and the Museum of Modern Art. Neither the division into scenes nor the scene titles necessarily correspond to either of the published scripts.

11. The French and Italian scripts, and several other foreign commentaries, refer to extensive klaxon or horn noises in this scene, but they do not appear in the version released in America.

12. See the citation and annotation for Bachmann (1963) in the bibliography.

13. Water, and especially the sea, are recurrent motifs in almost all of Fellini's films. The endings of *La strada, La dolce vita,* and *8½* are specific cases in which the director felt the need to make his final statement in a scene beside the sea.

14. I have used the word gratuitous throughout the text to refer to camera movements which are unmotivated by any movement in the frame. The word is not precise but it helps to distinguish such camera movements from those that obviously and deliberately follow some action that is taking place within the frame.

15. See the citations and annotations for Gill, Gilliatt, Pechter, and Walter (1964) in the bibliography.

16. In a film involving "mirror construction" (the English translator's term for Metz' *construction en abŷme*), such joking and other frequent uses of mirrors are an integral part of the film's structure.

17. The woman, Caterina Boratto, was a famous film actress in the 1930s. See note 30.

18. See the citation and annotation for Metz in the bibliography.

19. Although there seems to be no direct reference to the fact in the film, it is interesting to note that Claudia's last name is Cardinale. There are several similarities between Claudia and the Cardinal,

not the least of which is that each person is first a hope and then a disappointment.

20. There is a tantalizing shot in this sequence. At one point the camera zooms in on a hole in the wall of a building. The hole, as an idea of enclosure, is filled with matting that resembles the scaffolding of the spaceship tower, and through the hole one sees the ocean. Thus in one single shot, consciously or not, there is a mingling and identification of several motifs in the film.

21. See the citation and annotation for Moravia in the bibliography.

22. The English subtitles give only part of this important exchange. See "Special Fellini," *L'Avant-Scène du Cinéma,* no. 63 (1966), 48, 53.

23. See, for example, "Special Fellini," 67.

24. See note 8.

25. See the citation and annotation for Metz in the bibliography.

26. As other writers have often noted, in Fellini's films piazzas are frequently places of truth and revelations.

27. See the citation and annotation for Huss in the bibliography.

28. Best Foreign Language Film of the Year (to Fellini) and Best Achievement in Costume Design of a Black and White Picture (to Piero Gherardi). *8½* also won the New York Film Critics Award as the best foreign language film for 1963 and the Joseph Burtyn Award for best foreign film of the year.

29. The annotations in the bibliography provide a broad sampling of the critical response to the film.

30. One could also argue that Fellini has *deliberately* built on his past work, incorporating it within each new film. The relationship between the films would thus fit the imagery of dance and circularity (films which begin and end at similar places or with similar events) which occur so often in his work. Fellini, perhaps more than any of his contemporaries, also makes a similar effort to relate to the history of cinema, particularly the Italian cinema. There are many scenes of people attending the cinema. There appear in several of his films well known Italian actors and actresses—Caterina Boratto, Amedeo Nazzari (in *Nights of Cabiria*); and Polidor, the famous Italian comic who appears as a clown in several Fellini films. Fellini's love of the circus is certainly duplicated in earlier Italian films, such as Camerini and Zavattini's *Darò un milione* (1935).